OUR BELOVED FAREHAM

by

Alice James

PAUL CAVE PUBLICATIONS
LTD

Published by Paul Cave Publications Ltd.,
74 Bedford Place, Southampton, Hants

Printed by Brown & Son (Ringwood) Ltd.
Crowe Arch Lane, Ringwood, Hants. Tel: (0425) 476133

ISBN 0-86146-081-2

Published in September, 1991

Introduction

In my previous book, 'Fareham Between the Wars', I begged forgiveness for 'what I had left out' and promised to make amends by filling in gaps and recording more tales and memories before they were forgotten. With eagerness and generosity Fareham residents responded by positively swamping me with even more material so that once again I must apologise for 'what I have left out'!

I have attempted to fill in some of those gaps, added some more memories and have spread myself a little instead of confining the book to the period between the wars. Again, I have in part, followed many of the more important streets through Fareham as a guide to newcomers but I have also developed several themes and topics.

So, I shall now sit back (hopefully!), sort out the material yet unused and wait for even more to come in. I shall also expect the cheerful complaint 'you left out . . .' I hope that, in spite of the hard work, there will be a next time.

A.J.

Contents

Welcome to Fareham

Fareham, reading from past guides and journals, appears to have been a town which you either loved — or loved to hate. For instance, in 1878 it is described as 'a small but ancient and improving market town and port, pleasantly situated at the head of a narrow navigable creek', even if in the low lying districts the inhabitants were 'subject to the ague in wet weather'! Yet a writer fifty years later positively hated the town: 'A singularly unattractive little town with hardly any vestige of antiquity . . . the parish church of St. Peter is a strange building'!

Perhaps he felt a little like John Wesley, who two hundred years earlier had attempted to preach in the main street. Having left the loving people of the Isle of Wight, he records in his diary of the people of Fareham, 'Many gave great attention but seemed neither to feel nor understand anything.' Nor was his luck in twenty years later when he declared, 'A wild multitude was present', — doubtless the lads of the town, whose more recent descendants would declare 'Where's he from?'; 'Titchfield!'; 'Throw a brick at him!' In contrast *this* incomer (though admittedly not from Titchfield) has met with nothing but kindness and generosity.

In spite of its apparent size it is still possible to find the small, old Fareham with its delightful and independent old Farehamites who love the old town and hate the changes which time has brought. It is a privilege to be permitted to join this select band and put on paper their memories before it is too late.

So let us leave Titchfield behind and use the old road through Catisfield to Fareham, endeavouring to blot out of our minds the many new estates surrounding the area so that we can visualise the Catisfield to Fareham route of the not too distant past. Forget the by-pass (but don't get mown down in doing so!) and remember old Catisfield Lane and Fishers Hill. Here we find Catisfield House, home in 1955 of Mrs. Croucher. Previous owners had been Colonel Galt, Mr. Henry Leake, Mrs. Peel and Mr. G. E. Maltby. A sale of the Mount in 1985 produced a series of interesting photographs, some obviously of the house and grounds but all un-named.

At the top of Fishers Hill stands the house 'White Canons', home until 1956 of Mr. Bradly, ex-Headmaster of Price's School, Fareham.

Progress along the lane and here is the old 'Tin Church', as it was affectionately called instead of its true name, 'St. Columba's'. How many newcomers, I wonder, realise that the present St. Columba's is new? The church celebrates its centenary this year (1991). The old 'Tin Church' was much loved and served by such devoted people as Cdr. Ouvry, Warrant Officer O'Rourke and Mr. W. J. Shaw, and Mesdames Lawrence, Paton, Eldridge, Fletcher, Edney, Stretton, Roberts, Sait, Pink and Tyler to name but a few. HMS *Collingwood* made and gave the

Catisfield House today.

The 'Old Tin Church'.

weathervane — a ship looking not unlike the Mayflower, in 1956. Where is it now?

St. Columba's was a lively part of Holy Trinity parish with its Christmas parties, whist drives, dances, fetes and entertainments. The O'Brien legacy 'to the Aged and Needy' was still in existence and, with the help of the Rotarians, coal and blankets were distributed.

When the Tin Church was deconsecrated it became the ONE-O-SIX Club and one ex-choirboy of the 1930s, still apparently showing his loyalty to his old church, remembers standing on the exact spot where he once sang, to drink his pint. He also recalls that one Easter the choirboys went on strike having heard that the boys of Holy Trinity Church were getting free Easter eggs whilst they were not. The strike failed (according to this choirboy, the Choirmaster at the time seemed bigger than all the boys put together!). Corporal punishment in those days was not ruled out — even in church.

Leaving Catisfield Lane we come to the Avenue. Across the road at the corner of Peak (once 'Peat) Lane stands Heathfield House. It is best known by the people of Fareham as the home of the Stapleton-Brethertons (they arrived there in the late 19th century), although the house had previously had such distinguished owners as Major-General Hoare and Rt. Hon. Sir Thomas Aiskew, Bart. In the late 1920s, Mrs. Harvey was at Heathfield, but it was the Stapleton-Brethertons who left their mark. They were a much loved family who had lived in Catisfield before moving to Heathfield and were generous to the surrounding poorer families and who 'kept their servants' — always a good sign.

The family was Roman Catholic and on Sundays, Fareham waited for their 'turn-out' to arrive. With their three daughters and all the servants they were driven in a long, fine, shiny, black brake drawn by two horses. They were watched all along the road and no-one went into church until they had arrived. For a short time after World War II, the house was a branch of Lysses School, which had its main building at Lysses House in High Street, Fareham. Heathfield House is at present the Heathfield Manor bar and restaurant.

Many big houses with large gardens, such as 'Veryan', flanked the leafy Avenue and many were the garden parties, fetes and entertainments held in these gardens in aid of church and charities.

The Avenue, Fareham.

Catisfield in 1923.

Heathfield Manor today.

9

Blackbrook House (now a maternity home), the home of the Parker family for several generations, serves to remind us of the great Blackbrook estate which stretched on either side of the Avenue as far as Gudge Heath Lane and its toll gate. Blackbrook Cottage was destined to become Bishopswood, home for the bishops of Portsmouth. Again, 'true gentry', the Parkers gave loving thought for their poorer neighbours in the estates nearer the railway station. Food, wood and clothing went into these houses in the days after the First World War, when so many families were devastated by the loss of fathers and bread winners. 'One parent families' are no new thing.

Paxton Road seems to have had a remarkable community spirit, so many stories come out of it. Poor they might have been, but good neighbourliness combined with much humour created a complete community in which such people as 'Granny Pudge' and 'the Days' are quoted with affection by those who were children at the time. The children did play — marbles, skipping, hoops, tops and climbing on the backs of taxis (strictly forbidden) — but they also *worked*.

Mr. A. Swatton tells of a typical day when he was about seven. He was left fatherless after the war, and to help his mother he turned to his aunt who did laundry for the local gentry. She gave him the job of collecting and delivering the laundry baskets for which he would get the princely sum of two shillings a week and dinner on Mondays. On that day, he had to get a barrow and collect a hamper and laundry from the Bank (Lloyds). He had a metal hoop with which he used to run to and from school, he then rushed to collect the laundry, came home for lunch and rushed back to school. After school he was off to Catisfield to collect more laundry. Quite a day for a small boy, and he collected more laundry during the week. With four boys and a girl in the family, life could be said to be pretty hard.

There was humour also. His uncle used to work at the whiting works in Down End Road and he always walked to and from work. Although, his employers offered him a bicycle, he refused it. His wife laughed; for between Down End Road and home were the Delme Arms, the Bugle and the West End pub!

Another Farehamite tells of his grandfather, a tailor in Paxton Road, who would give him a penny to go to the corner shop and to ask for 'a pennorth of sweets and none of your b....y rubbish'. This he exactly repeated as he offered his penny. His grandfather was not very popular on his next shop visit! He also remembers one of the farmers bringing home incendiary bombs during World War II. These he gave to the children who used to let them off by dropping them. He recalls that his arms were often peppered with little burnt bits.

Blackbrook House Maternity Home.

The Avenue – the turning on the right is Gudge Heath Lane, just before the Toll Gate.
On the left is 'Redland's' garden.

Paxton Road.

With much affection are remembered the Miss Taylors at 'Croft House' with apples and pies for the children and baby clothes and a pram for a new arrival. There were many others with perhaps best remembered by that generation the Quarry family of 'Redlands'. They could never do too much for the children and last but not least, their magnificent turn-out on Sundays will always be remembered when the girls in the gallery at Holy Trinity Church (and also some of the ladies in church) waited breathlessly to see what magnificent new hats the Quarry ladies might be wearing!

Mrs. Sturmey, who died at the age of 103, was born in a tied cottage on the Parker estate. Her father was the pig man and she recalled that, as a child, she had to collect a bucketful of acorns before she went to school. Her father died relatively young and his widow and family were re-housed in one of the Cremer almshouses.

Two of the older inhabitants of Paxton Road, remembering their young days vouch for all the kindnesses received. Both Mrs. Hayter and Mrs. Race — and doubtless many more — remember the fairs held in Mr. West's meadow at the top of the road. All the fun of the fair, the steam engines and the gaily painted caravan belonging to Mr. and Mrs. Stanley and also the brandy snaps that Mrs. Stanley made. As children they used to store and look after bicycles for 2d. They also remember the circus which came along later in the season. The Quarrys left a small field in Redlands Lane for the children to play in

Titchfield Road looking back at Paxton Road.

but eventually it got sold and disappeared under houses. It was Mrs. Race, with her twin brother, who would hitch a ride (illegally of course) on the back of a cab when taking their father his dinner. Once she gave away her father's dinner to one of the men from the workhouse as she felt sorry for him.

The late Mr. J. P. Garrad came from a slightly better off family. His father was a coach builder at Young's which, in the days before the First World War, had its works under the viaduct near Portland Street. As a boy he too had work to do. At weekends he had to walk from the far end of Redlands Lane up to Blackbrook Farm for a gallon of so-called skimmed milk for 1d. (so-called because in recollection it seemed much richer than skimmed milk today).

Most people grew their own vegetables, which they sold by the gallon or bushel, usually 2d. a gallon. There was no hope of getting a 2d. cabbage into a basket; you grumbled if it was small enough to get your arm around it. If the large cabbages had gone, you usually got four for the same price.

Mr. Garrad remembered his mother wondering 'what the world was coming to' when a packet of one dozen *boxes* of matches rose to 1½d. Many matches, incidentally, were smuggled in from Belgium, hidden under the lawful cargo and landed at the Lower Quay.

13

Youngs, coach-builders, under the Viaduct Arches at Gosport Road, with the Creek and Harbour frozen over. The year? 1895.

Railways and other Transport

The entry into Fareham under the railway bridge was a narrow one and it was destined to remain a traffic hazard until the 1960s. In 1968, the old toll house, 'Redlands', and the cottages, together with the second West End public house were demolished. A new bridge was constructed and the road was widened.

Although now modernised and with the clarity of its entrance obscured by a large roundabout, the Railway Station and its forecourt remain much the same as in the past. Across the road the almshouses, Cremer Cottages, have been lost, as has the second West End pub, and the Tate's big house with its bow window. The building, which was once the Railway Hotel, still remains.

Sadly no longer do we see steam engines.

Fareham was always an important junction and particularly so when the area was strawberry growing country. Strawberries from as far afield as Sarisbury and Swanwick and the surrounding countryside were brought by train, cart and later, lorries, to be loaded on to the Strawberry Specials. So important were these 'Specials' that there was a potential revolution on the day that the Special was delayed because the royal train was coming through.

FAREHAM RAILWAY PORTER REWARDED.

ALFRED A. SWATTON, who has been presented with a silver watch by Sir Herbert Walker, General Manager of the Southern Railway Co., for brave and plucky conduct in rushing to the assistance of a lady passenger who had fallen between the platform and the footboard of a train, and holding her up till the train had stopped.

From time to time there were accidents on the railway, some trivial, some serious and some with loss of life. All were carefully recorded in an Accident Book. It must be remembered that near Knowle Hospital there is a bridge high above the line and falls (with deaths) are recorded in 1944. Many railwaymen have 'scalding' in the time of the steam trains; backs were strained lifting heavy goods; fingers were caught between luggage or in doors or when uncoupling vans and two unfortunate passengers suffered shock 'through suitcase falling on heads'. Twenty years previously, children were killed after climbing the embankment onto the railway line at the viaduct. More happily, in 1928, a young porter, Mr. A. A. Swatton, of Paxton Road, saved a lady passenger, who, attempting to alight from a moving train, got trapped between the train and the platform. That 'young man' happily still with us, received an inscribed silver watch for brave conduct.

15

The platform of Fareham's railway station crowded in anticipation of the arrival of Princess Henry at the beginning of this century. The appearance of the station has changed comparatively little since then.

The approach to the station in the 1920s.

Steam locomotive taking in water at Fareham station in June, 1953 (Coronation year).

This is 1958. Another splendid locomotive at Fareham.

Competition with the trains was growing locally. By 1906, the Gosport Tramway reached the Railway Terminus. It considerably speeded up the journey to Portsmouth if going via Gosport and the ferry — an adventure in itself. By 1921, Fareham had its own taxi rank, with motors beginning to replace the old horse drawn cabs. Although still named the Tramway Company, a bus service had also started.

Mr. J. P. Garrad, who left school at the age of fourteen in 1907, clearly remembered the changes that took place. He remembered the tramlines being laid in West Street in 1905/6, the traction engines pulling steam ploughing tackle and the man with the red flag. Coming out of school one day, the school-children stopped dead on hearing an awful noise. Looking along Gordon Road, they recognised young Dr. Case on a tricycle with noise and smoke coming from it and he was not pedalling. This was young Garrad's first sight of a motor vehicle of any kind. Then, in West Street one day, he heard a similar noise and along the street came apparently a bathchair. In place of a single wheel and handle at the front, the front rested on a square frame running on two wheels. In the centre of the frame was some machinery and a handle came out of the top of the frame turning backwards and was held by one of the occupants. The machinery banged and smoked and went 'tut tut tut tut', which perhaps was appropriate as the occupants were young Mr. Tutte and his father. They had made the machine themselves. Sometime later, a long low open touring car, with two big chains running over cogs to turn the back axle and banging loudly, chunked along West Street as the first real motor car. In it was Mr. Baker-White, who, with his brother and T.O.M. Sopwith, was at Seafield College, Hillhead. All three were to become aeroplane designers.

Dr. Burrell also had a noisy exploding motor bike and charabancs were becoming popular for day trips. 'Snobby' Goodall had one before the First World War and took some Fontley people up to London. Charlie Smith, of Fontley, started up the Fareham, Fontley and Knowle bus service in 1926. He started with just a fourteen seater, and by 1935 had three buses. Mr. F. Hoare said that Smith had competition from E. A. Millard, but secured the sole right from Knowle Hospital to pick up passengers on the estate. From 1929 he also got the contract to pick up the children near the waterworks to take them to the Fareham schools.

The village people gave the bus stops fancy names. The one near the church was 'St. Martin in the Fields', the ditch from Hope Farm to the droke was the 'River Nile' and the brickyard entrance was the 'Dockyard Gates'. The Miners' Arms was the 'Savoy Hotel', the hump backed bridge was the 'Marble Arch' and Corley's shop on the Knowle estate was 'Selfridges'.

Fontley hill was, and is, extremely steep. Clifton's lorries used to come up *backwards*. The buses all had wheel chains on during the snowy winter months.

West End, Fareham.

West End with the 'old' West End Inn (on the right). By 1968 the demand for action to ease road traffic congestion had reached such heights that the Titchfield Road railway bridge (see below) had to be widened and nearby houses pulled down.

The horse age was drawing to a close. There were frequently accidents when horses took fright when passing a noisy motor and even the Fire Brigade was once involved in a most complicated accident with a tram under the viaduct. Many were the cars and motorbikes which caught fire. Carelessness in overfilling the tank with petrol or fire occurring when the engine backfired were frequent. There seem also to have been some cases of 'spontaneous combustion for no reason' is given for fires in some garages.

Court cases dealt primarily on *speeding*, followed by careless driving. 'Hot pursuit' can scarcely have been the correct term for this period. One man was summoned for driving round a bend at 'a furious speed, estimated at 20 mph'; another 'travelling at the high speed of 15 mph' was apparently 'copped' when trying to get round a stationary vehicle near the Coal Exchange pub.

Also coming, of course, was the air age. Mr. Garrad remembered seeing an 'apparent' enormous box-kite flying from the direction of Portsmouth. Sitting in the centre was a man who proved to be the French aviator Paulham flying to the starting place to take part in the Daily Mail-sponsored race to Manchester. The war speeded up development and brought many flying heroes to the fore. In peacetime, Mr. F. Hoare remembers watching the Schneider Trophy race from his vantage point at the top of the water tower at Red Barns.

Now, after a period of neglect, nostalgia has taken over and enthusiasts once again can revel in the fine Shire horses, driving turnouts and not forgetting the steam traction engines and steam trains which were lost to us when the internal combustion engine took over.

Did she bring *you* into the world?

A familiar figure around Fareham was Nurse Cresswell. She came into the Fareham area in 1896 and before her retirement she lived for a time at Wallington before taking up residence at 138, Gordon Road. In the thirty years that she was with Hampshire County Council, she attended the births of at least 2,500 children, and at least 500 births before that! She attended mothers who often had 19 to 22 children in all and some of her patients had her services twice, at birth and when they became mothers. She was held in warm esteem not only for her skill but also for her kindness and patience.

Nurse Cressewell invariably used a tricycle on her rounds which included places as far afield as Rowner, Portchester and Southwick. In 1932 the residents decided that she should have a new one. A subscription list was opened, £25 was raised and she was presented with a new machine which cost £22 17s 6d. She retired in 1937 at the age of 70, and continued to live in Gordon Road until her death in 1947.

and where in earlier times, children went every morning to get a large bag of stale cakes for 6d. Neither is Church Path in its rightful place opposite Quay Street, nor does it cut through the allotments where children scrumped for apples. No longer does old Mr. Ireston have a butcher's shop at the corner of Trinity Street. He would call in any man he saw who was out of work and give him sausages or breast of lamb. Fortunately there is no longer a doss house in Cawtes Place and fortunately also there is no longer any danger of sewers overflowing in wet weather and flooding the living room as in the case of Batchelors the chemist. And yes, there *was* a candle maker, Mr. Strugnell. His shop was near the chemist. The smell from the boiling fat was terrible, no wonder it was known as the 'stink shop' by the children!

Batchelor's the chemist; closed in 1977 after 200 years as a chemist's shop.

The changing face of West Street . . .

West Street in Victorian times.

West Street in 1962 prior to any changes.

West Street – 1965.

West Street – 1920.

33

West Street – 1960s.

West Street – 1962.

West Street – 1920.

West Street – East End (1976-77).

Standing on the island between West Street and Union Street is Austin and Wyatt, chartered surveyors. In 1986, it celebrated 150 years of professional service. Thanks to Mr. D. J. (Michael) Swinburne, we have a record of the firm's history. It grew up from three generations of Richard Austins who lived and practised in Bishop's Waltham. (Telephone numbers B-W .3, Fareham .2). The first Richard Austin was an auctioneer and estate agent, but also (very sensibly!) the publican of the Crown Inn. He died in 1850 and ten years later, Richard Austin II had well and truly established the practice. By 1871, the firm having prospered, Richard Austin moved to a house which he had built on the Botley Road and known as 'The Thickets'. By now Richard Austin III, affectionately known as 'Dickie' Austin was also in the firm.

According to Mr. Swinburne, 1903 was a watershed in the development of the firm. It was then that the third Richard Austin went into partnership with young Archibald Wyatt of Fareham. In 1898 Archibald Wyatt was elected Secretary of the Fareham and Hants. Farmers' Club, an organisation with which he and his son, Stuart Wyatt, were to be associated for the following 82 years.

The practice continued successfully into the twentieth century with Dickie Austin, whose 'trade mark' was his silver-grey bowler hat which he wore on all occasions. During the First World War Archibald Wyatt served in the Hampshire Regiment. After the war, the partnership continued and was joined by a Mr. Warner. It was said that Mr. and Mrs. Dickie Austin were an attractive couple at the centre of the social scene and invitations to the splendid tennis parties were much sought after in the 'twenties and 'thirties. Sadly both partners died within a year of each other at the end of World War II.

During the following years, the practice continued to expand bringing in several partners whose photographs we show. After 1960 came the modern generation including D. J. Swinburne, Ian Judd, Graham Campbell, Nigel Gauntlett in the Fareham offices. Sadly, owing to the tragic death of James Wyatt in 1972, there are no longer any Austins or Wyatts in the partnership.

During its long history, the firm has gathered many traditions. We are told that until the early '50s there was only one staff car attached to the Fareham office — most staff used bicycles to carry out their duties as far afield as Hayling Island. All the staff in the Fareham office were obliged to form the labour force at the Fareham and Hants. Farmers' Club Show every Whit Monday and even into the '60s, staff working after 7 p.m. on settling the Fareham Market accounts were paid 2½p 'tea money'. The first job each day for Articled Pupils was to light the fires and fill the coal buckets!

This long association of the firm with the surrounding farming districts leads us inevitably to Fareham Market.

Douglas Gauntlett

Stuart Wyatt.

Blair-M. Warner

James Wyatt

Basil Gater

Geoffrey Mann

Richard Austin III.

Archibald Wyatt.

**The founders of the
modern partnership**

The Market

In my previous book, I mentioned the driving of animals to market 'on the hoof'. This was happening right into the 1950s although an increasing number were sent by lorry. I also mentioned Bill Hiscock and Jack Anderson, two of the original drovers, but here is a personal account of actual cattle drives as they occurred every Monday morning in 1951, as told by Mr. K. Shawyer:-

"Time, 7.30 a.m., any Monday morning, before school, some of the lads from Trinity Street helped in the great drive in great anticipation. The route was from Park Pond to Fareham Market via Trinity Street and West Street. I don't know why, but driving Mr. Etherington's cattle seemed to be better in the winter, but when it was cold and freezing, my mother's last words were 'Ken, if it's frozen, keep off the ice.' By the time we reached the pond (now part of Fareham Leisure Centre car park), Mr. Etherington had his cattle at the gate.

"Mr. Etherington's first name was Archie, and I confess that's what we called him when we were not in his or our parents' earshot.

"We all stood across Park Lane to turn the cattle to the right down the hill passing Price's School and the recreation ground. Half way down the hill, we overtook the cattle for the first job; we never had to worry over Northwood House on the left, for the dear old lady who lived there always had the large white wooden gates closed. So the first problem was Mr. and Mrs. Stockwell's cottage, because next to their home was, as is now, one of the entrances to the 'rec' and Colenso Road. (Mr. Stockwell was our local postman.) Having got the cattle past this point, we reached the Rising Sun pub. (now closed). The landlord, a big man and an ex policeman was Mr. Lockyer. He always stood on the steps as we passed. Across the road was a boot and shoe repair shop next to which was Mr. MacLean's big house. He was the school beadle and I remember the big iron gates to his home and the dares and double-dares to swing on it. Next to this house was a row of two up-two down houses (now the Youth Centre) then Mr. Meek's fish shop (now Trinity Fisheries). We had to get across the road to prevent the cattle from running up Gordon Road. Next to Mr. Meek's was a back alley to more houses. In place of the new carpark, road and gardens, there were houses with long gardens and on the end of the row was a tuck shop with its window in Trinity Street. It belonged to Mr. Plowman, who died from severe burns in 1962 when there was a fire in his living quarters.

"Opposite Mr. Plowman's lived a Mrs. Cawte and Mr. and Mrs. Sandy. They had a lovely brick wall. Until Mondays, that is! Every time we passed that

Opposite: Uplands House, built by Samuel Jellicoe. Sheep grazed in the grounds before eventually being taken off to the market.

wall the cattle knocked it over. They rebuilt it and it stood for another seven days. I often wondered if Mr. Etherington had to pay for it. After getting the cows out of the Sandy's garden we passed our house, with mother shooing the cattle away from our fence. Opposite our house on the left, was Mr. Hussey's sweet and paper shop. Next was Mr. Howard's fish and chip shop and following that Miss Self's vegetable shop. This is where the important job now came, to keep the cattle from crashing through the glass frontage of Mr. Jeffery's shop. It was here that one of us always got a foot trodden on!

"The main trouble with 20 to 30 cattle in a narrow road was not traffic. The leading cattle left deposits and those following slipped and fell down. Having got them past Jeffery's we had to block them off Russell's Place and then keep them on the road and not let them stray on to the bit of land in front of the Magistrates' Court; after all we did not want the magistrates treading in the deposits even if some of them were farmers. The deposits stayed until it rained or until what little traffic there was wore it away, and sometimes neither happened!

"We passed the Good Intent, ran ahead to the Royal Oak to stand across West Street in order to turn the cattle and then we were in West Street. It was wider and therefore easier to drive them past Mr. Etherington's farm house in Westbury. We had to stop the cattle from going up the steps of the Methodist church, prevent them from going into the bus station and miss Ernie, the paper vendor. Two of us stood at Portland Street, the rest across West Street and the cattle were turned into Portland Street. They went through the Portland pub yard into the market and were turned into the holding pens where they were weighed, given a number which was stuck onto their hide with a thick glue and then were sent into the back pens where they were auctioned."

Animals, in fact, poured in from the surrounding farms, some near, like bullocks from Dean Farm, some from long distances so that they rested overnight in fields around the town.

How much harder must have been the 'droving' when the beasts were driven 'on the hoof' after the market, to Portsmouth Central Abattoir?

This could never happen with today's *traffic* — what a pity!

An old document shows that in 1795, a public meeting was held to establish a market in Fareham and that the first market was to conducted on April 22nd which was a Monday. It was planned that from then on there should be a market every fortnight. This is probably the first attempt at an 'official market', for there were definitely earlier ones held at the bottom of High Street where Howard's House was the original old market house. This was the last house in the row of houses and shops which were once in the centre of West

Park Lane in 1920s and '30s. Below: Jeffery's before it was modernised.

Street. Obviously people were ready for trouble for there was a 'cage' or lock-up for malefactors. True there was an incident when someone made off with the key of the cage and a plea was made for its return! The numerous pubs and beer houses in the vicinity did a roaring trade as they were still to do in the 20th century. Some in the following list have disappeared: The George, Golden Lion and Coach and Horses in High Street; the Robin Hood and Little John plus many beer houses in Union Street; the Red Lion, King's Head, King's Arms, the Crown, Bugle, White Hart and the Lamb all in West Street between High Street and Portland Street.

Before the First World War, West Street on market day was crowded with people, animals, farm carts and wagons. There were herds of cattle, frequently over a hundred head of cattle loose in the street. The market company was relatively young and many of the older farmers and dealers could not see the point of paying someone else to sell what they could sell themselves. So, although they took advantage of the fact that it was market day, the farmers kept the cattle bunched up along the south side of the street.

Fareham's inhabitants always seem to have been prepared for any eventualities which might occur. After all, it only livened up the proceedings. Certainly the number of beasts escaping and charging all over Fareham seems to have been above average and certainly left a deep impression on anyone in the vicinity. A handy lamp post was sometimes a useful safe refuge! Mrs. Race remembers shopping for her mother on one market day when a bull went wild and ran down West Street. "I never, ever, ran so fast," she said. No doubt many others of the older generation have their own memories similar to those mentioned in my previous book.

The bustle and excitement of market day communicated itself to all and especially to the children. Many were the boys who kept an eye open for the truant officer. People had their own favourite part of the market, for there was a wide variety of animals and goods. Poultry and chicks, pigeons, rabbits, kittens and puppies were all in their small pens. There were vegetables, fruit and eggs for auction apart from the main market pens of cattle, sheep and pigs. Watching the auctioneer was fascinating but completely unintelligible to the outsider, of which the author was one. I am afraid that I loathed the pens where young calves were kept, roped and bundled closely together with sometimes one down on the floor and unable to rise. There never seemed to be inspectors around, and nobody seemed to care. I was, and I admit it, squeamish, so I kept away. Yet I was not the only one. To young Mr. Shawyer it was a puzzle that a kind man like Mr. Pink who bred special pigeons called 'tumblers' could use a tool looking rather like a giant nutcracker with sharp needles which was used to pierce and thus mark the ears of the pigs. He hated the squeals and the bleeding, and this was in the 1950s. Despite this, to the layman, apparent cruelty, it was essential to mark the animals to establish ownership.

Above: Fareham Market in early 1900s; below: in 1973.

The market place is now a car park, as desolate as it used to be at night. It is apparently destined to be covered by yet more shops linking up to West Street where many buildings have already been demolished. The end of another piece of Fareham history.

Once the Market Place – now a car park (1987 photograph).

The South East Hants Association

This Association was in being in the early part of the 19th century and the offices of Messrs. Austin & Wyatt held a very long, extremely decorative notice for the period 1838. It is impossible to reproduce in typing the sheer beauty of the printing, but the notice ran as follows:-

South East Hants
ASSOCIATION
For the encouragement of
INDUSTRIOUS AND MERITORIOUS
AGRICULTURAL
LABORERS

44

The President was H.P. Delme, Esq., the Treasurer was James Thresher and the Secretary was Charles Osborn. The plan was to introduce a series of awards for various classes of farmers, agricultural laborers (*sic*) and cottagers who have used their land to the best advantage, brought up their families with little or no parish relief and who have also helped families in the case of sickness or death. There was also to be a grand ploughing match at Cams Park on the morning of the annual meeting. This meeting was inevitably held at the 'Red Lion' with 'Dinner on the Table at Two O'clock'. By happy coincidence, I obtained over thirty years ago, a copy of the annual meeting held in 1838. We therefore have a record of the successful candidates, all of whom had to be regular attendants at Divine Worship and not frequenters of Public Houses or Beershops! The Hampshire Advertiser refers to the amount of good already done since the formation of the Association three years previously. There were thirty-two competitors in the ploughing matches which included a competition between the men of Hampshire and Sussex. This particular year the Hampshire men won.

Some of the premium winners were as follows: Abraham Marshall, aged 51; £5 for having brought up nine children with only £5 parochial relief. Anthony Lambert, aged 45; £1 for having brought up five children with only 7/6 relief, 'although he had been put to considerable expense by the sickness and death of five children and two wives.' Thomas Tull; £5 'he has saved £80 during his father's lifetime. He annually gave him a pig and a sufficient quantity of wood. Since his father's death twelve years ago, he has paid his mother's house rent.'

These and many other awards were made at the annual dinner held at the 'Red Lion', Fareham 'where about a hundred gentlemen and farmers sat down to one of those excellent dinners for which widow Harris is so justly famous. Mr. H. P. Delme presided and on the removal of the cloth a very choice dessert was placed on the table; the wines were excellent.'

'The Chairman called for a bumper to the first toast, The Queen (drunk with immense cheering). The next toast was received with similar enthusiasm — The Queen Dowager. The distribution of the premiums followed. The hale and joyous countenance of the successful candidates, their clean and comfortable dress and respectful yet animated manner in which they received their well merited awards was delightful. A toast was drunk to the health of the successful candidates.'

All awards having been given, the meeting got down to the business of drinking toasts in earnestness. Toasts were now drunk to the Bishop and Clergy of the Diocese and to the Lord Lieutenant of the County. These were duly acknowledged and were followed by toasts to the Army and Navy and to Agriculture in all its branches. The health of the President was now proposed followed by one to the Judges of the ploughing.

Hilarity was now setting in (can one wonder?). And the toast to the Secretary and Treasurer was proposed (laughter and cheers). Mr. Thresher rose to state that he would actively discharge his duty by dunning them most excessively if they did not pay up their subscriptions (loud laughter and renewed cheers). Toasts to the Vice-Presidents and to the Committee and Stewards were now drunk and the Hon. E. T. Yorke., M. P. for Cambridgeshire, 'in excellent voice sang The Old English Gentleman'. Applause was tremendous and a toast to The Old English Gentleman was drunk.

The health of Mr. Gage 'whose character was modelled on that of The Old English Gentleman' was now drunk and was followed by one to the health of Mrs. Delme. Mr. Lane sang a song which was highly applauded and toasted. Several other toasts were done ample justice to, and the party on breaking up expressed themselves as 'highly delighted with the whole business of the day'.

So they should have been. After a minimum of eighteen toasts plus the excellent wines at dinner, one does wonder how some of the members got home safely. Mr. H. P. Delme was a notable whip, regularly seen driving his matched team of four greys around the district. I hope he took his coachman that day.

Not Mr. Delme with his wife up – but the late Tom Parker, Mrs. B. Dyke up, and his four matched bays.

Osborn Road

Lying parallel and above West Street is Osborn Road which is now continued through into Trinity Street. Old Charles Street, containing the Police Station (now the Registrar's Office) was to become the southern part of Osborn Road.

Osborn Road was owned together with most of the land to the north of West Street by Charles Osborn. He planned to have a road of large houses providing a vista to the parish church and a new route to it and to the school. Church Path was to be left open to meet up with the droke also leading to the schools. Plots were allocated for new vicarages for both S.S. Peter and Paul and Holy Trinity churches. These were the first two buildings developed. Much of the land to the south of the road remained open as allotments until recently and this land was part of the old medieval fields of Fareham. Some of the land became tennis courts and later other houses were developed.

It is amusing to record that when the houses were developed it was discovered that the land between them and the road belonged to the Bishop of Winchester, and access (no doubt at a price) had to be obtained.

It is with the allotments that we are chiefly concerned in this chapter. The period is in the late 1940s at a time when Mr. Kenneth Shawyer was five years old.

'Every Sunday, unless it was raining, the first thing my father did was to fold a potato sack, put it over the crossbar of his bike and I sat astride it. I can still remember how painful it was by the time he reached the Rising Sun (later the Sun, now closed) a distance of about 200 yards from our house in Trinity Street. The pain was relieved when we walked the alley past Northwood House. At that time the house and grounds were still in their full glory. There was a long black fence and inside stood high sturdy beech trees. There was much wild life in the garden and many wood pigeons and cuckoos. My father could call the wood pigeons to within 20 feet of us and he could also bring down the cuckoos although they never came so close. My dad taught me the skill, but I am only half as good as he was.

Back on the crossbar we turned right down Harrison Road and left following the flint walls of Osborn Road. The big trees that were part of the flint walls are almost completely gone. On our right were the tennis courts (now the Post Office car park) and just before we turned right at the entrance to the church, there was a large field (now car park and Ferneham Hall). At the end of the field there was a clump of blackthorn trees, heavy with ivy where nightingales sang just as it was getting dark. Having passed the trees we reached the allotments, each of which was made up of a certain numbers of 'rods' (a rod = 5½ yards). There were four family plots next to each other so it was quite a family gathering every Sunday morning.

It was on a hot Sunday morning when we were cutting grass under the great walnut tree that my father who was using a bill hook told me to call my uncles as he had cut himself. My uncle Bill jumped the hedge to find that my father's finger was nearly hanging off. My uncle wanted dad to go to the doctor. 'No, pass us that baling string!' I watched as my father bound his finger back together again — the string was soon bright red. 'At least you're not royal, Alf,' joked uncle Bill, and Uncle Joe said 'good job it ain't your throat.' They were all laughing and I did not understand the laughter and neither did my mother when we got home. He refused to go to the doctor and I often saw him change the string. Then one day I noticed that he had no string on his finger. 'Good as new, boy,' he said, and wagged it at me and he never did have any more trouble with that finger.

A few years later when we were at the allotment, we found that Uncle Bill had put up an Anderson shelter. 'I'm going to grow mushrooms,' he said, packing in horse manure as if there was no tomorrow. Each week we asked, but after seven weeks we found him in a temper, throwing out all the manure and some of it came onto our plot. All was forgotten for another three weeks. Then one morning when we arrived at the allotment gate, I said 'What's all that paper, dad?' 'That's not paper, son, they's mushrooms'. Dad picked me up and said 'Look at uncle Bill's, it's white like a blanket!' An hour or so later Uncle Bill arrived. 'Do you want to buy some mushrooms, Bill?' said my father. Then Uncle Bill noticed his plot — it was pure white. 'All that b....y work!' he said. We were giving mushrooms away for days and we always did claim that no-one could grow mushrooms as well as uncle Bill could.'

Remnants of the old allotments still exist, I hope that the Hampshire characters do so also.

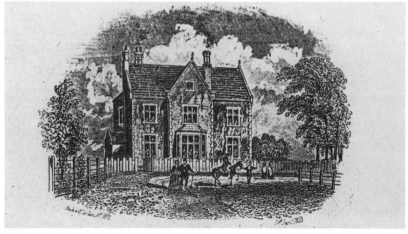

Trinity Parsonage House

Osborn Road showing houses built on the original Fareham Farm.

Church Path, 1937.

High Street and its surroundings

Having reached the 'Red Lion' — a pleasant stop — we have many routes of interest to follow but for the moment we will consider High Street and its surroundings. Of those surroundings, at the town end of the street is Union Street, which was the notorious 'red-light' district of Fareham (or perhaps one of them!). Union Street is so called because the Union Workhouse was once there. It is a short street but it was notorious for its beer houses and pubs — the two best known being the 'White Lion' and the 'Robin Hood and Little John'. Saved by the efforts of Mr. J. C. Draper, Union Street now presents a very different face to the world although it is still possible to see one doorway to a Jug and Bottle department and a huge archway where coaches and drays could pass through.

High Street, described by David Lloyd as one of the finest Georgian High Streets in the south of England, has been and still is the subject of many pictures. Yet it must be remembered that High Street is not all Georgian; there is mock Georgian, Victorian, Queen Anne, Tudor and modern. However, it blends together well and thankfully we still have it, for the western side was under threat from development in the 1950s.

The Barney family of 'Lysses' was the driving force behind many of the changes and in the building of fine houses. In course of time, the 'George' and the 'Coach and Horses' were to disappear, but the 'Golden Lion' together with much older cottages are still there. It must also be remembered that it was a busy street occupied by both gentry and non-gentry for tucked behind many houses were cottages reached by drokes from the High Street. At the turn of the century, no fewer than 35 business premises are listed including shoemakers and dressmakers, a butcher, a fishmonger, baker, sweet shop, a cycle store and a furniture store. On the general picture we can see Warn's drapery shop and Edney the corn merchant. Nearby was Croad's builders yard due to form the basis of a business at 6a High Street, (at the end of a droke!) which was to continue until recently.

Rose Neath, a large house at the top of High Street, was for years the home of the Steward of the Cams estate and was connected to the cottages next door by speaking tubes. No. 64 and No. 67 High Street were occupied by doctors. No. 64 was destined to have a doctor's practice until well after the Second World War. No. 67 was reputed to be haunted until a skeleton was dug up in the cellar during the 1930s. No. 69 High Street was originally a School for Young Gentlemen many years before it became Wykeham House School for Girls. At Kintyre House, Admiral Donaldson held sway over the road in front of his house, sending for the police should a car be parked there for more than half an hour. The relative peace of this part of the High Street was greatly disturbed by the great Cheese Fair held at St. Peters-tide on the last two days in June. It was not an official holiday and many and bitter were the complaints made by the school teachers about truancy.

Red Lion Hotel.

Union Street, 1967 – the door of the old pub, 'Robin Hood and Little John' is a few paces on from the baby carriage.

High Street long ago.

High Street, Nos. 68-71 – 1964, showing the County Club, Wykeham House, Stable and Kintyre House.

Bottom of High Street (Nos. 77-80), 1962.

Top of High Street – autumn, 1982.

This street has also been the home of many important people. We must not forget Sir John Goss, born at 21, High Street and visits made to that same street by William Makepeace Thackeray and Charlotte Yonge. The latter's book, 'A Reputed Changeling' is based in and around the area. At No. 12, the house 'St. Giles', lived the mother of Arthur Lee, who was to become M.P. for South Hants. and to rise to become Lord Lee of Fareham and to present 'Chequers' with its 1500 acres estate and many works of art to the nation for the use of the Prime Minister. When M.P.s were voted salaries he assured his local constituents that he would never collect his as he 'regarded it an honour to represent them'. Cynics may declare that 'well, he was married to a wealthy heiress', but to read his biography is to make one realise that here was a man of principle and not privilege, much strengtheneed and supported first by his mother and then by his wife.

An old Farehamite, Mr. P. Shaughnessy, writing from Kingston, Ontario, Canada, remarked how surprised he was to find Lee so highly regarded in Canada as 'he had hardly heard of him in Fareham'. A case perhaps of 'a prophet is not without honour save in his own country'? Lord Lee had in 1940, presented his valuable collection of 16th century silver to Toronto University together with other valuables and pictures to Kingston Royal Military College. The final link was broken in 1966 when Ruth, Viscountess Lee of Fareham, died at the age of ninety-two. A man often forgotten who Fareham should remember.

Proceeding northwards down High Street, once known as Vicar's Hill we come to the old vicarage which stands opposite the church gates. The old cottages which flank the path to the gates have now gone, as has Holliday's dairy and the shops on the corner of Osborn Road. However, we still have Hansford's, the old cycle works.

We must also remember — even when referring to High Street — that Fareham was primarily a port with absolute high water mark above Wallington bridge. The Mill Pond was at the bottom of some of the gardens and flooding of those gardens was a frequent occurrence. I fear also, that many of the inhabitants of those houses had knowledge of passages leading down to the river and that smuggling was not confined to the lower orders at the Quay! 'Brandy for the parson, baccy for the clerk' did apply as the author was once told by a ninety-year-old who once lived in High Street. Lysses Path also leads directly to Bridgefoot and the water.

We all have our favourite houses in High Street. The author's is, inevitably, No. 69, with its magnificent porch, entrance hall and sweeping staircase — down the bannisters of which, it must be admitted she once saw a member of her staff slide from top to bottom!

Arthur H. Lee, M.P.

The front door of No. 69 High Street.

Wickham Road and the Workhouse

Leaving Fareham by the High Street and passing old Wallington Hill we come to a Post Office and a row of terraced houses built on land which was once fields and known as Hog Plat and which is part of the original Manor of Fareham. The terrace ends at a public house called the Travellers Rest which is separated from the old Junior School by a droke. This droke is one of several in the area, short cuts leading inevitably to S.S. Peter and Paul church.

A little further along on the left are two almshouses erected by a Mr. Joseph Paddon in memory of his wife. They are still in use although over one hundred years old.

At the junction of Old Turnpike and Wickham Road is a garage, an interesting building as much of its structure contained unwanted pieces of stone from the local stonemasons including headstones planned for World War I cemeteries which were broken during engraving or had engraving mistakes. A gap between the garage and the Beehive Cottages marks the spot where the Beehive public house stood. It was kept by Mr. E. T. Cummings, licensed retailer for beer and tobacco. Near here also, were the original Turnpike toll gates, for Old Turnpike Road itself was the original Turnpike road. Prior to that, it is named on maps as North Road. When the new turnpike was put through as Wickham Road, the gates were moved on to the new turnpike as shown in the picture. The Workhouse and Chapel can be seen in the distance and old Doctor Case sits in his pony and trap.

It is interesting that the A32 is still called 'the Turnpike' to locals up the Meon Valley, certainly as far as Droxford.

Old Turnpike Road still has many of the cottages used by the workers in the brickyards and also in the clay pipe factory. One of the old cattle pounds also still exists. At the top of the road is the Turnpike Inn, originally the 'New Inn'. The older 'New Inn' was further down the road.

To digress for a moment, I do wish the breweries would stop changing the names of their public houses. How can an *Englishman* (or woman for that matter) give strangers adequate directions without being able to rely on the names of pubs! More seriously, these changes are already beginning to cause problems when dealing with local history as did the changing road names in the district.

The top of Old Turnpike marks another old junction with Park Lane (already mentioned), North Hill which once had the old potteries as described in 'Fareham Between the Wars' and Kiln Road, its very name indicating the past industrial history of this area.

Turnpike Tollgate.

The older 'New Inn' was further down the road.

57

Along Kiln Road there is an interesting row of houses, reputed to have been put up by Napoleonic prisoners of war. These houses, really only small cottages, were owned by a Mr. Bugg. It was inevitable that the cottages should become known as 'Bug's Row' and the gap between the cottages was 'Flea Pit Alley'. In the 1960s the row was destined to be demolished as unfit for habitation but it was saved by intervention and the cottages were turned into attractive dwellings (one of which is called 'The Magnolias').

Most of the land between Old Turnpike and Wickham Road consisted of clay pits for brickyards and potteries owned by Mr. Sandy, in fact his house is known as 'The Potteries' and with its five acres of garden built on the old clay pits, linked both roads. The gardens were thrown open for fetes and garden parties.

'Bug's Row', Kiln Road (1961).

An early Fareham motor-bus.

'Fareham folk on a day trip in a charabanc (photograph courtesy of T. P. Yoxall).

West Street looking towards the centre of the town.

West Street showing 'Admirals Row'.

The Butcher, the Baker,
the Candlestick maker

It requires considerable imagination for the newcomer to attempt to visualise the lovely approach to Fareham along West Street from the West End. A few small shops, yes, but mainly a leafy, tree lined, wide street with big houses. No signs of high rise apartments, used car lots and garages so reminiscent of the entry to any small town in an American 'movie'!

Much of West Street was dealt with in detail in my earlier book 'Fareham Between the Wars' published in 1989. Places not then mentioned in detail are (hopefully) now to be dealt with.

It must be remembered that King's Road did not appear until after the First World War and that, although Blind Lane had been widened to become Hartlands Road, it still led to the big cricket field by Holy Trinity Church.

West Street near Osborn Road corner. This photograph must have been taken before the First World War because on the right-hand side there is no entrance to King's Road.

On the West Street in front of that field and opening were several old family shops, among them, Birk's the furniture store, which was established in 1912. Also there were the Portland Dairy and J. T. See's, now the office of 'The News'. Nearby was the original Foresters Hall and across the road was the Fareham Drill Hall, re-named the Connaught Drill Hall. Lusby's and Pyle's had second shops in this part of town and Stone's was a wonderful family grocers.

There, right in the centre of the town, were still big houses, with large grounds and still surrounded by fields. Westbury Manor, home for 'oceans of Admirals', offices for over 200 years of the Stewards of Fareham Manor and later the home of Fareham Urban District Council, is now happily restored as the Westbury Manor Museum.

Westbury House and grounds lying opposite were not so lucky. There is still a Westbury Passage and a Westbury Farm but the big house, where in the 1920s and 1930s a Mr. Tyrrell remembers spending holidays with his grandmother, Mrs. Matthews, has been pulled down. The gardens were magnificent with every kind of fruit including a great mulberry tree, lawns and a tennis court. Part of the site is now occupied by 'McDonalds'.

Progressing on was Jeffery's furniture store, a family firm still to be found in Fareham (Schreiber Centre) and Gosport. It is interesting to remember that

Trinity Street junction with West Street – in this photograph (taken after 1914-18 war).

Stone's, the wonderful family grocers, and its 1948 staff: Muriel Wells, Marjorie Bone, Connie Warner, Winnie Early and Joan Bell.

small buses and coaches were parked in the middle of the street and that the large Methodist Church was not demolished until after World War II in order that the bus station could be enlarged. The late George Privett in his book 'The Story of Fareham', comments on the destruction of the three houses next to Portland Street. One of them was the holiday home for William Thackeray. He states 'One of the never-to-be-forgotten blots on Fareham's escutcheon is the permission given by its authorities for the demolition of the historic building in favour of an omnibus station.'

One wonders what his feelings would be now. Not only has that group of houses disappeared, so also have most of the houses in Portland Street.

Westbury House, seen from Portland Street – between the Wars.

Westbury Manor (in the 1970s).

The magnificent Embassy Cinema in West Street (on left hand side).

In 1983 the Embassy Cinema was demolished. Some of the interesting 'relics' are now in Westbury Manor Museum.

Although the 'Portland' remains, the 'Toby Jug', houses and shops have now gone as have Solomons mill and grain store. There was another corn store at the back of Portland Chambers for many years, hence the old name 'The Corn Exchange' sometimes seen on prints of the building.

From the top of the street, the isolated Roman Catholic church may now be seen and if we look over the footbridge at the bottom of the street, the Market Place is still an open space and car park.

The series of advertisements (dated 1938) for past family firms will, I feel sure raise a few memories. Dodges, the drapers; Letherens, the general store; Staceys the ironmongers; Busseys and Burts, the butchers; Waters the fishmongers; Vimpanys the jewellers and watch repairers; Suttons the bookshop; Phillips the outfitters; and Haywards the greengrocers, to name a few. No longer can we find Pyle's restaurant and cake shop at the end of Church Path (often better known as Pyle's alley) where we once gathered for 'elevens'

Portland Street Hall and cottages (one a lending library)
the second house was the home of Thackeray's great aunt.

28

The Potteries.

This brings us to the Workhouse, now St. Christopher's Hospital.

There had been tremendous changes in the Workhouse in the latter part of the 19th century. The Board of Guardians were an extremely dedicated set of people, not averse to meeting even at Christmas should an emergency arise. And emergencies did arise. There is for instance the well documented case of a certain Master going 'into an inmate's room on several occasions to put out her gaslight!' The resulting illegitimate child led to the instant dismissal of the Master and Matron. Much in fact rested upon the Master and Matron. Food in the 19th century was plain and by our standards, sparse. Yet it compared well with that of the 'deserving poor' as Sir William Cremer, M.P., was to testify in Parliament. On paper at least, the Cremer family came off worst. Sir William was born in Fareham and the father deserted the family. Educated by his mother, he rose to be an M.P. and later a Nobel Peace Prize winner. He left land and money for the building of the Cremer almshouses, which were near the railway station. Sadly they were demolished when the road was widened.

Much of the material on the Workhouse comes from Mr. 'Monty' Worlock, son of the last Workhouse Master. His personal reminiscences follow in the next chapter.

Entering from the Wickham Road, the Master's offices were on the right and the Porters' room on the left. Another entrance on the left led to a large yard where female tramps had their quarters. A big conservatory and corridor led from the hall to the kitchen, boiler house, cookhouse, dining hall and scullery together with entrances to three more yards. These were all ground floor places and also included the women's ward, the stores, nursery and committee rooms. The chapel was on the south side. At the front of the first floor was the infirmary taking in two wings. In the centre there was a flat occupied by the Master and Matron, always a married couple. Behind the central flat were the sleeping quarters, needlework rooms and old ladies' rooms.

At the back there were coal sheds, a cobbler's, a painter's shop, a gardener's shed, a big airing ground for the old men to sit out and a large day room for the very old.

The procedure for any person wishing to enter such an establishment as an inmate was first to see the Relieving Officer who would give them a ticket of admission to take refuge in the Workhouse. Future inmates had to be very poor indeed, out of work and often homeless. On arrival they were put in the Receiving Ward, bathed and clothed and given a clean bed. They were issued with standard workhouse clothing and also with a Sunday suit. Next day, they were examined by the Medical Officer and if they had come in with an ailment the doctor would send them to the Infirmary. If they were fit they were sent to an able bodied section and found a job of work. Men and women were treated alike but were separated. Both were divided into able bodied or old and had separate day rooms. They were encouraged to find work.

With tramps (vagrants) it was somewhat different. They walked from workhouse to workhouse and a tramp coming in for the night had to hand in a small ticket to say where he had been the previous night and state where he planned to be the following night. They were given a bath and their clothes were fumigated. If they wished to stay for a day, they were locked up in the Stone Cells to break stones. If sick, they were sent to the sick ward to be looked after.

The female side was Matron's domain as was the Infirmary. They were housed in the same way as the men and were involved in cleaning, sewing and in the laundries. Occasionally a young girl would come into the workhouse, generally unmarried, to have her child. For this there was a special small clinic right at the top of the third floor. Mothers were allowed to keep their children until they were three years old. They were encouraged to find work and to take the child with them, otherwise at three years of age they were sent to the orphanage in Portsmouth. Such was the position when the last Master took over.

Born in the Workhouse

W. M. Worlock, Master, Fareham Poor Law Institution, 1911-1931.

Mr. and Mrs. W. M. Worlock took over as Master and Matron of the Workhouse on December 11th 1911, from Mr. and Mrs. Tuck. They were to be at the Workhouse until 1931 and were therefore the last Master and Matron. Their son 'Monty' was born in 1914.

The Worlocks found Fareham Workhouse in a semi Dickensian state. All the walls were whitewashed, inmates' facilities were primitive, much needed to be done and worst of all, Christmas was only a fortnight away and nothing had been prepared. Mrs. Worlock had a tremendous time organising all the cooking and kitchen chores involved and that Christmas was one of the best for years.

Any improvements which were made had to receive the sanction of the Board of Guardians and improvements came rapidly. The place was stripped down, whitewash was done away with except in the tramps' ward, walls were painted with good colours and the Master had the carpenter put in a lot of panelling which was nicely painted. Floorboards were stained and polished and within a year the place was as clean as a new pin.

'Monty' Worlock now continues:-

The war, of course, was now in progress and I faintly remember my first Christmas decorations when I was about three. Earlier, there had been a Zeppelin raid and my mother told me that when the Zeppelin came over, she took me down to the Workhouse cellar. However, in Fareham, the Zep caused a Police Superintendent to get on his bike and ride through West Street yelling 'Air raid, keep calm, keep calm'. As he passed Aubrey Pyle's bakery, a man called Larry Shilling who was visiting, opened a window and yelled 'Why don't you go back to the Station and put your trousers on?' The Super had been riding his bike with just his police jacket and no trousers; just his long john pants.

During the war, the people of Fareham used to put on concerts which were appreciated by the inmates. I well remember Miss Jewell who often came to the Workhouse and played the piano to entertain the inmates. Later on, my father organised the Workhouse Concert Party.

Although young, it was impossible not to appreciate the problems of the poor people who entered the Workhouse. So often, they were simply 'down on their luck' and my parents did all they could for them. Tramps were a different matter, some of them could be quite dangerous and I never got to see any of those tickets. The Stone Cells had been converted into coal bunkers before I was born. My father considered them degrading and instead put the tramps to work in digging, sawing wood or any other odd jobs.

Improvements came steadily. Sleeping wards and day rooms were beautifully painted. Heating was by steam radiators and coal fires. In one of the men's yards, my father had a fountain built. I wonder if it is still there? Mentioning the steam radiators reminds me that when I was about seven years old, we had as a Workhouse handyman a rather dubious performer in the arts of handiwork. His job was to ensure that the two vertical steam boilers together with the multitude of steam pipes and coppers were kept in good working order. The boilers used to be stripped down every three months in order to clean the inside and get rid of the chalk fur. It was a slightly leaking steam pipe that caused the furore. The big boiler was being chipped and the little one was on stand-by. Their steam outlets both went into the same pipe and the valve leak in the outlet of the big boiler caused scalding drops of water to fall on the heads of the men doing the chipping. This could not go on!

So the handyman had a great idea. He got a barrel cask bung, put sacking over it and banged it into the outlet of the big boiler. It stopped the steam leak, but he forgot all about it. The men finished their chipping, came out through the manhole and the boiler was sealed up for the next three months, supposedly. What happened next could have been disastrous. At five-thirty next morning my parents were woken by frantic shouting and a roaring noise of steam. The flat was just above the boilerhouse. My father forgot to put his trousers on and came down three flights of stairs in his pyjamas, rushed

Workhouse Concert Party 1920-21. Town notables include Mr. Watts (back row 3rd from right), Mr. Hunt (Borough Surveyor, 3rd from left), Mr. Worlock (extreme left, back row).

through the big kitchen to the boilerhouse to find the big boiler's safety valve was 'doing its nut'. The steam pressure was one hundred per square inch and no steam was escaping to the cookers or anywhere else. The boiler had, of course, been sealed up by that bung. The fire was raked out, a lot of cold water was injected and when it had cooled enough the manhole was unsealed and the bung was taken out. It was a near thing and I slept through it all!

With the Board's sanction, new bathrooms were installed and the gardens were brought up to standard. The gardener was first class, he was one of the old inmates who used to work for Sir John Davidson at Cams Hall. All the fruit and vegetables were grown in the Workhouse grounds and there was also a piggery. No pork was ever bought for the kitchens.

In 1924, a house was built on the land by the Chapel for the Master and his family. Here we stayed until 1931. The house, built of bricks from Mr. Sandy's brickyard across the road, is still there.

I spent many happy hours as a boy playing games with the 'old chaps' — skittles, dominoes, darts etc. Of course my father, being musical and a

In picture: Mrs. Warlock, Messrs. Stratton, Heath, Dr. Oliver (in front), Crockford (behind), Rogers, Houghton, Hammond and V. T. Keen. Mr. Warlock in doorway. Work House Guardians — 1928-29

marvellous organiser and teacher, quickly got together a concert party consisting of inmates, staff and even Guardians. Shows were put on and Fareham people also entertained with concert parties (as can be seen from the photograph on page 63) and singing groups. Young people, like the Scouts also did their part.

There is the old joke about 'Christmas Day in the Workhouse!' I've had quite a few of them. They were marvellous. All the Guardians would come up and serve in the Dining Hall. The inmates would all sit together at big long tables and have a meal of roast pork, vegetables and Christmas pudding. The men would also have beer. In the evening my father would put on the Christmas show in which we all performed. The inmates then retired, the Dining Hall floor was french chalked and there would be a dance for townspeople, friends and relatives of staff and the dance would go on into Boxing Day.'

So much of this is confirmed by Mrs. Clifton who was for three and a half years Cook General Assistant. She saw more of the female side of the establishment. She confirms that in the 1920s there was always plenty of food but as much of it was steamed, it tended to be dull. But there were hot dinners, 150 pork loin chops in the ovens at one time!

All the inmates were well looked after and she remembers the sadness of the children having to be separated and sent to the orphanage. She also remembers the Hunger Marchers. They stayed in workhouses overnight as they made their way to London and they were passed from workhouse to workhouse. The previous workhouse gave short notice and there was panic stations. Soldiers' straw beds were borrowed from the Drill Hall and put down in the Dining Hall. There were about 180 and staff prepared two huge iron pots of hardboiled eggs, sausages and bacon and the Porter was cutting bread for two hours for bread and cheese and they were also given hot cocoa. They left about ten the next morning having been not the slightest trouble.

Mrs. Clifton left to marry but went back, first as a temporary measure but then to stay four years as Assistant Matron. She too, speaks with appreciation of Mr. Worlock, kindly, a wonderful organiser and teacher and an excellent comedian on the stage.

On March 11th, 1930 the Board of Guardians went out of office under the Local Government Act.

The Port of Fareham

'The river leading to Fareham within a mile of the town is an absolute good and safe place to moor ships and in all respects as convenient and safe a harbour as Chatham. £2,000 may be saved to the King in moorings and men.' So runs part of a letter written to Sir John Coke in 1630.

Yet Fareham had been an important port for merchant and royal navy as well as a boat building centre for many years before that letter. With a tide rising over 12 feet it was possible for vessels of up to 300 tons to moor at the quays and there was a floating dock capable of holding vessels up to 500 tons. Such a port and harbour could at times compete with Southampton, for it was a free port, trading in the 14th century in wine, wheat and timber. In Tudor times the timber was moved in vast quantities from Fareham and Titchfield Parks and brought in from Redlands Lane at a charge of 5d per mile. These shipments were destined to continue right into the 17th century and most of it was bound for Chatham. Fareham was recommended 'to secure it from being used elsewhere'. It would appear that some of the timber was going astray! In fact, a certain captain complained that private men were buying it and that he had seen 'all the best trees docked for buckets, which would grieve anyone to behold'.

There were in fact many quays. Lower Quay, Town Quay and Upper Wharf could be said to be continuous. Many old Fareham residents insist that the Upper Wharf was always known as 'Itch-y-boo' or 'Hitch-a-bow' corner. The spelling probably varies according to pronunciation. This area was a very lively one with a pub known as the 'Drum and Monkey' frequented by sailors and smugglers, and Hewletts Court described as a den of iniquity, vice and immorality by the Vicar of Fareham! The Excise men, were of course, about a hundred yards away at the 'Chequers', a fact which seemed to bother the smugglers not a whit! The Lower Quay had its own quota of pubs, beer houses and smugglers. One particular family definitely linking up with the Parish Church with its nefarious activities. (We do not know whether the Vicar was involved or not, but it does seem possible.)

Other quays included what became known as Bathing House Quay, further up the river. It was so called because a bathing house was built here in the 19th century with 'two large baths for males and females, supplied from the river at high water and with hot and cold showers'. It was then that the road to the quay changed from Park Lane to Bathing House Lane and in more modern times to Bath Lane. Higher still up the river there were quays by the tide mill and along the shores of Wallington — but more of them later. Downstream from Fareham were Salterns and several smaller quays, all trading, all boat building and doubtless, all with their own private activities. (Poaching on the Cams estate being one of those activities.)

The Quay.

Junction of East Street and Bath Lane – originally Bathing House Lane, which led to the public bathing houses on the Quay (now Gashouse Quay).

As time went on, the type of trade slowly altered. Timber was still exported together with bricks, tiles, corn, sacking and rope, chalk and whiting, and leather. Red pottery 'extensively manufactured by Mr. Stares of Wallington, together with pots, jars and pipkins' had become an important export. Coal was brought in on flat bottomed barges by such firms as Woods the coal merchant who had their yard behind the 'Coal Exchange'. Later Fraser and Whites brought coal to the Upper Quay.

Upper Wharf (in 1966) – grain, sand and coal ships used the wharf.

Coach builders shipped their carriages abroad. Messrs. Pounds and Garrads built and exported carriages from their works under the viaduct arches, where there was a convenient smithy and wheelwright. The most important coachbuilder was Coles of West Street, (coachbuilders to William IV) who sent carriages to Australia and other parts of the world. It is interesting to record that they were fined seven shillings and sixpence for blocking the carriageway in front of their shop which one would have thought was a rather difficult procedure considering the width of West Street! That same factory was to become Hinxmans and later Wadham Stringers, thus continuing the tradition well into the 20th century.

Gradually the Creek was silting up so that dredging became necessary and the Upper Quay was less used. The predominant trade was now in bricks

The Fareham winter in 1895 was so severe that the Quay was iced up.

and tiles from the extensive works all over the area. As this industry was dealt with in detail in my earlier book, it will perhaps suffice to remind the reader that Fareham Reds were used in the building of the Albert Hall, the interior of many of London's municipal buildings and even the Town Hall at Capetown, South Africa. It was a sad day when bricks were *imported* from Belgium. It is to be hoped that the smuggled matches *under* the bricks proved a small consolation! Fontley tiles continued to be exported until the Second World War. Loading a barge with tiles took an entire week with lorries running continuously from 7 a.m. until 5.30 p.m. or noon on Saturday.

Silting up continued so that the Town Quay went out of use and the war years marked the end of Fareham as a large trading port. Timber from Scandinavia, coal, sand and gravel continued to be brought to the Upper Quay. Trade was further hampered by a series of cold winters, for example that of 1895, as seen in the photograph, when a large fair was held on the ice and skating both there and on the Mill Pond became very popular pursuits. The author also remembers the bitter winters of 1962 and 1963; the creek froze and boys were cycling on it, a coal ship was endeavouring to break through the ice using crane and bucket and the upper reaches resembled a scene from Scott of the Antarctic.

Trade, of course, meant boat building as also did the proximity of the Navy. Generations of boat building families are recorded; the Burrells, the Fritchetts, Hampers, Sees and Chippendales are familiar names bringing us right through to modern times when Fareham was said to be the largest small boat building port on the south coast.

The first record of boat building for the Navy is the 'Marie of Fareham', built for Henry IV. Remnants of details remain for the 'Marie'; 'they are to take a ballinger at their discretion and mariners (pressed men) so they may be ready by October 1403'. But human nature never changes and in February 1404 is recorded 'pardon to John Lyle of the Marie, who with others stayed so long at Dartmouth that their victuals and other goods were expended!'

In the 16th century a ship called the 'Jesus' was built on the shores of the creek. In fact, due to constant wars with Dutch and French, the Navy was taking a greater interest as time progressed and boat building was continuous. It was during the 17th century that prisoner of war hulks began to be moored in Fareham Lake and a hospital was established in an attempt to alleviate suffering. Ships were ordered to be washed down with vinegar, smoked and tarred inside and out for the better cleansing of contagious distempers from the West Indies. (A modern doctor's comment — 'useless, but the ships would smell better'.) Fresh provisions were ordered for the men but much was in vain, for as one captain commented 'of the 60 men put ashore sick, not above three have returned aboard'. Meanwhile the Hospital Fields behind the Lower Quay collected their bodies, lying three deep. The Parish church has many records and memorials to officers and men of the ships. Resolution, Cambridge, York, Fairfax, Lyon, Rupert, are names that ring down the ages as do Eagle, Kent, Revenge and Swiftsure.

In 1805, a few weeks after Nelson's death at Trafalgar, Lord Collingwood proposed the erection 'at the expense of the Squadron, on Portsdown Hill a memorial to their late chief's memory and great name'. Contributions came in when the prize money was distributed; the first stone was laid in 1807 of Nelson's Monument on the hill close by the later Fort Nelson.

With peace, ordinary civilian work took over with the building of fishing boats, trading vessels, yachts and power boats. A regular ferry service ran from Fareham to Gosport. An annual regatta was held and a Sailing Club came into being. This was much supported by Messrs. Stedman, See and Garrad. The doings of the Sailing Club we will leave until we write about entertainments in Fareham. One of Fareham's vicars, the Rev. Berthon was responsible for inventing the 'Berthon Boat', a collapsible, folding lifeboat. Of the modern boat builders, Mr. See was probably responsible for more innovations than most. He turned his attention to speed boats and was responsible for the construction of the speed boat in which the Hon. Mrs. V. Bruce was to break the cross channel record. He was also responsible for putting compasses in his speed boats. Having experienced the incident when one of five speed boats hoping to cross the channel, fetched up on the Essex coast, this probably filled a long felt want!

One of Mr. See's speed boats.

Messrs. Hampers, with boat building yards at the Upper Wharf and in Mill Road, must not be forgotten for the quality of their hand constructed yachts.

It must be said that the Navy was capable of causing a certain amount of chaos and sometimes irritation and amusement in some of its practices. For instance, in 1866, during gunnery practice in HMS Excellent, four conical shells, each weighing 110lbs., fell in the neighbourhood of Portchester. One swept over Wicor Farm House exciting excessive alarm in the inmates. Two others fell on land belonging to James Martin of Cams Farm and who happened to be on horseback at the time and in the vicinity. The result, although not disastrous, was somewhat embarrassing to the gentleman concerned. George Privett also tells the true story of the owner of Cams Hall lodging a complaint to the Admiralty because he feared target practice might result in the damaging of his flower beds. This was not to be tolerated, and the officials winked at the manner in which it was dealt with. Under cover of darkness, some young midshipmen rowed up the creek carrying a cannon ball. This they laid under the drawing room window of the Hall, dug a furrow behind it and left. The following morning the owner of Cams, seeing the cannon ball, felt his worst fears had been realised. A cannon ball had entered his very domicile, or at least, was near enough to lodge an objection. He lodged another complaint, but regrettably history does not tell us the result! Fareham, however, was much amused.

Cedar Cottage

72

Bridgefoot and the Mill Pond

If, on leaving the 'Red Lion', we continue eastwards down East Street we pass several large houses, Burpham House and Fareham House being two of them. The former house was once the home of the much respected Mr. E. Goble and Fareham House, home of the naval family of Loring for generations, was also for a time the home of Sir Roger Keyes, R.N. It now has a new lease of life as the home of Wykeham House School and has changed its name to Wykeham House which will doubtless cause much confusion to future local historians.

On the other side of the road, Fairfield House with its extensive grounds has disappeared, Yew Tree Cottage being the only surviving relic. The house was the home of the Deanes, commemorated in Deanes Park Road. For a time there was Cedar Cottage, later Cedar Garage, but this too, has now given way to modern buildings. It was said that the cottage was originally the centre for the piggeries of the big house!

From here, the road descends rapidly to one of the most historic parts of Fareham, wantonly destroyed in the name of progress. Here, at Bridgefoot we now come to a great roundabout instead of the historic Mill Pond. The old tidal mill was lost in 1919. Straddling the creek it took advantage of the incoming tides and captured water in the vast Mill Pond. This pond was sometimes called the 'Mill Hole' by the inhabitants of Fareham. Water could be released when required and the overflows came through outfalls under a bridge at Bridgefoot. Elderly residents of the Mill remember it well, the children from one family were actually bathed in warm water from the Mill Hole and the boys of another used to dive into the deep water from the upper windows of the Mill House! Now all that remains is a concreted outfall for the river and a plaque in the wall by the viaduct to remind us of history.

The old quay at Cams was destined to remain until the 1960s. It had been much in use for trade in corn and was also much used for the bringing in of material for road repairs. East Street and the old A27 were, it has to be admitted, quite tricky to negotiate. There was a sharp bend at the bottom of the hill in order to cross the rather hump-backed bridge over the outfalls and this was to be followed by a sharp turn in the opposite direction past the 'Delme Arms', once the 'Horse and Groom', to get up Cams Hill. Many were the cars which failed to negotiate that first bend and ended up in the water. Weekends were particularly popular!

The first change came when old Cams Hill was abandoned and the A27 was straightened and its gradient eased. Cams Hill became an attractive backwater and its steepness no longer a hazard for cars and buses on cold wintry mornings. The Cams estate, having earlier lost fifteen acres for the new Fareham Girls' Grammar School, now lost a further minimum of fifteen

Cams Mill.

Bridgefoot with Fairfield House in the background.

Bridgefoot, Fareham   PN1452

Cams Quay.

acres and its two lodges at the entrance to the estate. The lodges were lived in by one family, daytime accommodation in one lodge, bedrooms in the other! An interesting point now arose for it became obvious that there was in fact a straight route from Fareham via Lysses Path, across the bridge and pointing directly through to Roman Way, Portchester and the Castle. We all looked hopefully but in vain for signs of a Roman road in the school grounds.

Then came more changes. True, the Mill Pond had silted up badly and become very marshy but it did help to hold surplus water during very high tides, thus controlling some of the flooding. The course of the river was changed to the Wallington Shore Road side and was partly canalised. The rest, together with the bridge and the old quay all disappeared under rubble to become a giant roundabout. To many drivers the roundabout is probably more tricky to negotiate than the original double bend and it is certainly easier to get lost on it! Regrettably, water has to go somewhere and flooding still occurs along the Wallington Shore Road and in Wallington.

In the past, the Mill Pond could be the centre for recreation, sheer mischief and even fury. It was customary for it to be drained on St., Peter's Eve and the inhabitants were allowed to collect the fish and eels. One person made off with a swan and exited rapidly pursued by the village constable! As the marshes grew, one inhabitant of South Wallington attempted to regain land by fencing it. Fury erupted, fences were thrown into the Mill Pond until he

The old Cams Mill.

desisted. Fury also erupted when an 'unjust steward' of Cams attempted to close access to fishing in the Mill Hole by putting up a gate. Twice the gate ended up in the water, scurrilous lampoons were written, and a 'guy' was 'strung up' under the viaduct and a crowd, preceded by the town band (doubtless the lads of the village) marched up to Rose Neath in High Street, the home of the steward, broke all the windows, marched down to the Mill Pond and again threw the gates in the water. This time, however, the town lost, as the land did belong to the Squire.

The Pond was a pleasant area for recreation and social activity. Swimming, boating and fishing were pleasant pastimes, an annual regatta was held and in severe winters there was skating with skating parties for the gentry. It has to be recorded that an elderly resident of Cams Hall was taken on the ice in a rocking chair by her son-in-law, with unfortunate consequences for both parties — but no doubt to the amusement of many — when they went through the ice.

Somehow it did not seem strange to the author when, one Monday morning, the sixth formers of the Grammar School came in bursting with joy when the first crane and dredger began to sink in the mud of the Mill Pond when the changes began. After all, they were the descendents of those original Farehamites!

Above: Cams Hill and the old lodges (right) at the start of the construction of the new road.
Below: The Mill Pond had silted up badly.

Wallington

The last chapter linked Fareham with Wallington by the Mill Pond and Wallington Shore Road. It could also, of course, be reached by the very steep Wallington Hill. In the early 19th century, the Hill had a large island in the middle of the road making it even steeper than it is in modern times. Until mainly closed to traffic nowadays, it was once the bane of many learner drivers who prayed that they would be able to turn into the main road without having to do 'standing start!'

In spite of being constantly referred to in directories as 'a hamlet with a brewery', Wallington, although small, was a thriving settlement surrounded by rich farm land and including valuable water meadows. It also had three very important industries, Mr. Stares potteries to which we have already referred, the brewery owned by the Saunders family which was to remain in operation up to 1944, and the Tanneries. As industries faded, Wallington for a time became increasingly residential, but industry was again to develop, this time around Broadcut.

The river and mill pond were important both for industry and trading. Unfortunately, the village has suffered continually from flooding; roads and houses are flooded far too frequently. An article in 1861 comments that 'the Wallington stream was swelled to an unusual height, which being greatly increased by the heavy tide, the waters were flowing at a fearful pace. Much damage was done to Messrs. Sharland's property and to the surrounding houses, the inhabitants having to take everything upstairs'. This type of flooding still happens, although Broadcut is not flooded to a depth of three feet!

It is not possible in a book of this size, to deal fully with such a delightful area. In fact it merits a book in its own right. The author therefore apologises, in advance, for omitting some of the subjects which may be dear to Wallingtonian hearts.

Mr. Vernon Lees has recently completed a model of the village as it was in 1866. There were several large houses, sited in equally large grounds, which were the homes of people who were not only of local importance. Regrettably, most have now been demolished. Wallington House can claim the younger brother of Admiral Patton who having served first with the East India Company, was for many years the Governor of St. Helena; Captain Collingwood Dickson, RN, who was living there in 1852; finally the Coppinger family, the last owners of the house. One ancestor was Dr. Coppinger who took part in the Nares expedition to the Arctic and was on board the 'Discovery'. The house was destroyed in 1967. Other houses and their families included the Paddons at Wallington Hill House, long time solicitors in the district; Mr. Norton at Wallington Lodge and the Sharlands at Purvestor House.

Wallington House (23 July, 1967).

Purvestor House – home of the Sharland family.

The building of the forts on Portsdown Hill was also destined to change many features of life both in Wallington and Fareham. Fort Wallington was being built between 1861 and 1874 and a light railway was built to carry up the essential materials. Obviously with troops at the fort, there was increased trading and the women of Wallington did the laundry! The early arrival of an Irish regiment did much to increase the tolerance towards Roman Catholics in the community; the priest did much good in the town and brought about the eventual possibility of the building of the church in Hartlands Road. There were two public houses in Wallington, one, the 'White Horse', happily still flourishes. A new pub was to arise, the 'Fort Wallington Tavern' now re-named the 'Cob and Pen' and thus losing another connection with local history, even if it has some connection with the natural history of the local area. Many people will remember Mr. and Mrs. Wellman, mine hosts of the 'Fort Wallington Tavern'.

Much of Fort Wallington was destroyed in the 1950s and 1960s. It was sold and there were certainly two somewhat eccentric events which occurred. The first was when the owner declared U.D.I. from Fareham and had a banner stretched across the front of the fort to proclaim the fact! The second was when the next owner decided to turn demolition expert and surrounding houses

Below: Mr. and Mrs. Wellman.

80

St. Edith's Home for Girls (1929).

and gardens were bombarded with bricks and rubble! It took a court case to settle that problem. Nowadays it is amusing to read advertisements welcoming one to the 17th century 'Dungeon Club', especially as the buildings were not due to go up until two centuries later.

Another feature of Wallington was St. Edith's House now disguised as the 'Roundabout Hotel'. Originally an Industrial Home for Girls between the ages of 14 and 16 years, it was established in 1869 by Lady Larcom and was transferred to the Church of England Society for Homes for Waifs and Strays in 1884. It was rebuilt in 1907 as St. Edith's, there were usually twenty girls who were trained to be servants for housework, laundry work and cooking. Subscribers to the Home, reads the notice, 'can have servants from the Home', a useful perk! Happily its status changed as the years advanced although it has been admitted that even their schoolmates tended to 'look down' on the girls. Let us, however, turn to Purvestor house, the Sharland family, and the Tanneries using a series of photographs, much overdue for publication and given to the author by Mrs. George Privett.

There had been tanneries in the area for several centuries. The first recorded is owned by the name of Rolfe, in Stuart times. There is still a Rolfe's Mead in Wallington. The next important tanner comes from the Thresher family who had in fact intermarried with the Rolfes. The Threshers prospered and were closely connected also with the parish church and with the town of Fareham, providing clergy and magistrates and linking up with the old Manors of Fareham. There then arrived on the scene an 'incomer', Mr. Edward Sharland together with his family. This family was to be closely linked with Wallington and the parish church well into living memory. The tanneries stood approximately opposite Drift Road and Purvestor House (with its windows of quarter inch plate glass) was noted for its beautiful gardens which extended at the back as far as Broadcut. There was a right of way through to Broadcut and many are the stories told of the mischief which the children got up to around there — for what is more tempting than forbidden territory!

The Sharlands expanded the industry and gave much local employment, bringing in men from North Fareham and Fontley and also employing girls in the house from the same areas. Extra labour was taken on during the Bark Harvest, the bark was stored in hovels or stacked in the open until required. Valencian nuts were also used to assist in the staining. The hides were bought and brought in from long distances and the excellence of the leather became known all over England. Some hides came by wagon from Southampton, the horses being driven by a Mr. Holden. Many of the hides were brought directly to the quay. They were taken to the lime yards prior to the 'fleshing' or removal of the hair. They then went into the first tan pit with a solution of bark and Valencian nuts and they were moved from pit to pit for several months. It was dangerous work for the walks between the pits were narrow. The hides were then hauled out, cut into shape, rolled, pressed and dried to make the eventual leather which was rolled up and tied by a so-called 'Tanyard Knot', a double reef knot. At peak periods about 250 hides were processed weekly requiring 1,200 tons of bark and 100 tons of Valencian nuts.

The tanneries also had a farm keeping beef and dairy cattle and poultry. The food was excellent. Oxtails were to be had and each employee was given one quart of skimmed milk daily. There were regular festive dinners with festive feasts for workers and the family at harvest and Christmas and also 'summer treats' for all the families of the employees.

As many people will know, Mr. Sharland was responsible for saving the Parish Church from fire. At that time (1844) Fareham Farm with its fields and barns stood next to the church. A fire started at the farm, spread to the barns and the heat started to melt the lead on the church roof. Mr. Sharland organised a rescue operation and ordered that all the wet hides should be brought up from the tannery to cover the roof and walls of the church. His efforts were successful.

Old Mrs. Sharland was known to the village as Queen Victoria! Two well-known employees were Mr. Brown who was in charge of the boilers and Mr. Collins who had the unenviable job of flushing out the tan pits. Each pit had to be flushed out three times and Mr. Sharland used to hand out a shilling for each one.

The Sharland family.

The pictures on this and the following pages were taken by photographer W. R. Hogg, of George Street, Ryde, and form a part of photographs collected by Mrs. George Privett.

One of the Sharland daughters with Purvestor House and the Tannery in the background.

Preparing for steaming at the Wellington Tannery. Mr. Norris (foreman) in the foreground.

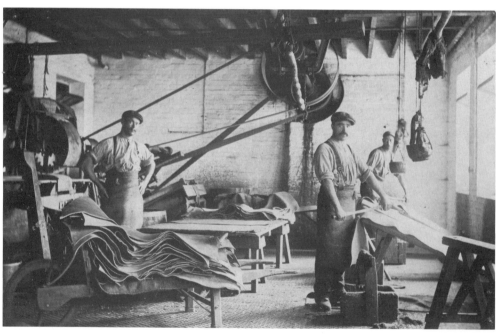

In the stretching room – employees (left to right) – Mr. Withers, Mr. Cox and Mr. Cummings.

Bark stores with Mr. and Mrs. Evans.

Tannery families. On the far right are Mr. Norris and his family.

Wallington Tannery employees – and (below) employees on their annual outing.

Mrs. Sharland

It was a sad day for Wallington when the tannery was sold in 1913. It remained idle with the pits full of water for several years when it was bought by a Mr. Evans. When it was re-sold, Fareham Council hoped to buy it but they were beaten by the villagers. Mr. Collins bought the meadow, Mr. Luckett bought the meadow on the other side of the tannery and Mr. Pounds, the tanyard. Mr. Evans bought all the leather at 2½d per hide. Later he sold it at 3d making a vast profit because there were tons of it.

During the Second World War, the tannery buildings were taken over by the A.R.P. Later they were used for storage and now little is left of any original building.

We must remember, that as these industries were fading, other local firms were building up to take a valuable place in the community. The Collins, Clifton and Luckett families are but three of those which will be remembered in future Wallington local history.

Sports (By special request)

I am most grateful to Mrs. S. (Phelps) Smith, Mr. M. Privett and Mr. H. Sturgess for the rather precious sports photographs and articles which they have loaned. I am particularly grateful to Mr. Sturgess for his phenomenal memory!

Represented mainly are cricket and football although there are also some hockey and tennis photographs. School teams will be shown separately.

Cricket was always an important game for Fareham and a match of Fareham versus Purbrook is recorded in 1845 when Fareham won by one run. The first cricket field was in the Southampton Road area approximately where Harrison Road is situated, but the land was sold off for development in 1871. Another cricket field existed on the big recreation ground near Holy Trinity Church. This field was used for general recreation, fetes and other jollifications. The Fareham Cricket Club itself, was founded in 1882 and a committee chose the team colours, claret and light blue stripes. It is amusing to record that the opening match was played between married and single members — the latter fielding fifteen players and winning by six runs! There is incidentally a story, that in later years it was not unusual for Havant to slip twelve players onto the field when playing Fareham.

The cricket field had its pitch by what was then Wheeler's wood yard and the railway ran close to it. On one occasion a spark from the engine set fire to the thatched roof of the pavilion.

Fareham Cricket Club temporarily faded out in 1902 and tenancy of the cricket field ceased. Fortunately, another team called the 'early closers' was in existence and decided to take over the name of Fareham Cricket Club. Matches now were played on what was to become Bath Lane Recreation Ground. The First World War inevitably broke the sequence, but in 1919 games were re-started and fortunately none of the team members had been lost. There were so many up and coming youngsters that a second XI was started, which in fact managed to defeat the first XI for the cricket was of a very high standard. Fareham frequently won the Gosport League Championships. In 1931 they gained exclusive use of the No. 1 pitch at Bath Lane, the council letting it to them for £5 annually. The same year, the Fareham Brotherhood's Wednesday XI came to an end and the Cricket Club took over the fixtures.

One of the smaller delightful local cricket clubs was 'the Eskimos' founded in 1929 and playing on Broad-Halfpenny Down opposite the 'Bat and Ball'. The team always played the Actors on New Year's Day and on their first match the game was interrupted as the entire Hambledon Hunt crossed the pitch! Play was adjourned to the 'Bat and Ball' and as a result of this event, a badge showing a red fox was adopted.

It is not possible in a book of this size to give full details of all the sports played, although there is much more material available. Suffice it to say that

Fareham, the Fareham Brotherhood and most of the boys' schools had strong football teams. Hockey, tennis, athletics all had thriving clubs which had been begun in the later 1800s. As we look at the programmes, we also see that many of these sports had a family tradition for the same names crop up time and time again. These names can be seen under the photographs.

It is possible in the pre-war years, that Price's School tended to dominate because many of the boys stayed on into the sixth forms and were thus able to furnish outside teams with up and coming young players.

Nevertheless, other schools had their teams and many of the members supplied local clubs. Both boys and girls at the Church of England Junior Schools and those of the Secondary Modern Schools had excellent teams in various sports. So too did Wykeham House School for Girls. Knowle Hospital staff had a fine football team in the 1950s.

It must, however, be said that from the 1960s there were fewer organised compulsory games. Price's had under 13s hockey and cricket XIs. There was an increase in many other activities, for example, swimming. Schools had grown large, having well over 600 pupils, transport had become more difficult as pupils were at schools on the outskirts of the town. It is interesting to note for instance, that at Fareham Girls' Grammar School, the time of school closing was actually dictated by the availability of the school buses! As these buses brought the children into the town centre they then frequently had further long journeys to make in order to get home and it became increasingly difficult to have many school activities except in the lunch hour.

Since World War II many other alternative attractions had grown up. The cinema was very important and Fareham, with its two cinemas, was putting on four shows a week. It was easy to get to Gosport or Portsmouth and television was a fascinating newcomer. There is also no doubt that the young people had more freedom and more money and seniors were taking Saturday jobs. The character of schools was also changing, in some schools 'competition' was almost becoming a 'dirty' word. Expeditions and field trips usually in school time, became important.

In all fairness it must also be said that the moving forward of public examinations also took its toll. Pre World War II, Higher School Certificate and Matriculation examinations were held in July. These days, G.C.S.E. and A Levels are liable to start in May and drag on for several weeks making match fixtures very difficult.

However, Price's, turned into a Sixth Form College and co-educational, did keep up the sports and activities as may be seen in their annual magazine. They had a devoted staff built upon the senior staff of both schools to which the author, then a Trustee, must pay tribute. There is not room to go into details or include extra photographs but these are being held in reserve!

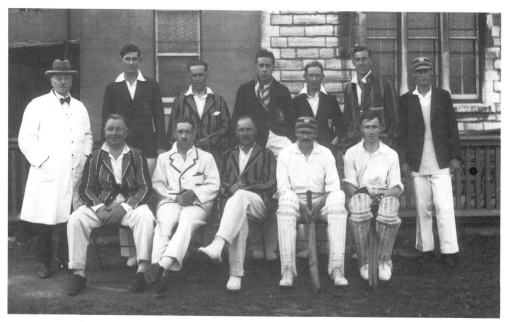

Fareham Cricket Club – First XI – 1928
Wyatt, Smith, Sinnott, Connell, Norman, Lamport,
Pyle, Palmer, Bennett, Budden, Sturgess.

Cricket Cup – 1935
Back row: L to R. 5th and 6th H. Sturgess, B. Phelps, 9th Shaw. Middle row: L to
R. 3rd Newbury, Cribb, Carver, Troke, Norman, V.G. Croad (panama hat) who presented
the cup.

Fareham taking the field in the 1950s.
Players include J. Browning, H. Sturgess, G. Collins, with Scott, T. Wagstaffe and B. Phelps in front.

Fareham Cricket Club in the late 1950s.
Back row: L to R, Packer (umpire), Hart, Clancy, ?, Browning, Rands, Bennet, Newell (scorer), Boot (umpire). Front row: L to R, Basford, ?, Phelps (captain), Freemantle, Jeffery.

The First Fareham Tennis Club
*Taken before the First World War. Identified are: Mr. Gale (extreme left), Mr. H. Privett
(sitting left), Mrs. R. Dyke (extreme right) and Mr. D. Phelps (centre back).*

And Football. . . Fareham Brotherhood First Year Team 1926/27 and officials
*Back row: Tatham, Bone, Clark, White, Lewis, Dick, Primmer. Centre row: Hill, Sturgess,
Sir William Parker, Bart., Carter, Legge. Front row: Jackman, Saywell, Wassell, Locke.*
*Mr. Tatham entered a team for the Brotherhood Cup before Fareham had one! Next year,
the team won the Meon Valley Division Two Shield, the Nicholson Cup and the League
Tournament Cup. Sir William Parker, of Blackbrook House, holding the Shield, was President
of the Fareham Brotherhood.*

Fareham Brotherhood First XI – Winners of the Brotherhood Cup. Played at the Dell, South-ampton. Back row: L to R, Hobbs, Hill, White, Legge, Lewis. Centre row: L to R, 3rd Clifton (with rosette), Saywell, Goodall, Carter, Lamport. Front row: L to R, Cummins, Sturgess, Saywell (captain), Phelps, Brace.

Fareham Brotherhood First and Second XI with officials at Bath Lane Recreation Ground, Fareham – 1935

Fareham Town Football Club – Post World War Two?
Cup winners – Phelps (now manager) standing on right.

Knowle Hospital Football Team – 1952/53
Back row: Watts, Ings, Cunliffe, Robertson, Fillingham, Everett, Parslow, Burr, Stone, Smith.
Front: Holland, Kingswell, Carter, Hoare, White, Whitear, Jannaway. Photograph includes officials. The team won the Meon Valley Division 1 in their first season in League football.

LONDON SOCIETY OF OLD PRICEANS – SUNDAY HOCKEY TEAM, 1936.
In blazer: A. S. French (friend of 'Dumps'). Left to right, back row: Buckley, Masterman,
Barnes, Wellbourne, White, Gregory, Hayward, Lardean. Front row: Phillips, 'Dumps', Apps.

FAREHAM HOCKEY TEAM – 1950
Back row: Newbury, Moore, Sturgess, Hawkins, Tuck, ?.
Front row: Wagstaff, Riches, Lewis, Powell, Neal.

FAREHAM HOCKEY TEAM – Late 1950s
Back row: Mogridge, Newbury, Tuck, Phelps, Wagstaff, ?.
Front row: Bennett, Holt, ?, Neal, ?.

PRICE'S SCHOOL FORM VA – 1924
Back row: Cook, Jones, Andrew, Bussey, Forsyth, Collinhome, White, Sturgess. Middle row: Goodall, Moore, Ditchburn, Mr. Shaddock, Edwards, Blanch, Hayward. Front row: Hall, Elcock, Cawte, Cummins, Phillips, Houghton.

CHURCH OF ENGLAND FOOTBALL TEAM – 1933 (Cup Winners)
Back row: Hedaker, Barrett, Mott, White, Neale. Middle row: Wheeler, Chase, J. Crouch,
F. Crouch, Wassell. Front: Durham, Frost.

GIRLS' BOARD SCHOOL NETBALL VII – 1934 (Runners-up in Netball Cup)
Back row: Gamblin, Adamson, Miss Jackson, McDonald, Colwell. Front row: Walker,
Colbourne, Robinson.

Opening day, 1956

The staff – July, 1957

Schools and their Activities
(mainly in pictures)

In 'Fareham Between the Wars' I dealt in some detail with the growth of schools in the area and was able to mention the loss of one historic school, Price's, which had been founded in 1721. After World War II there was much rebuilding and expansion in schools and there arose a new school, Fareham Girls' Grammar School, in 1956. Sadly it was to have a short life as a grammar school but it nevertheless played a great part in the education of girls who previously had to travel to Purbrook or Gosport for their senior work.

Miss Lowe, the first Headmistress, recorded her feelings when, on a black cold day in 1956 she trudged up old Cams Hill, took a short cut across the copse and found a hockey field. She crossed the rutted track which was later to become the drive and got her first glimpse of the long line of the South front of the school. Workmen were everywhere and apparent chaos reigned.

Nevertheless, staff had to be appointed for the school which would for the moment have first and second year pupils and would have to share rooms with 148 second form girls from Fareham County Secondary School for two years. All went to work, timetables were made out but all plans underwent another change in November when Wicor Primary School was partially burnt down and 128 boys and girls became guests for the term. One form had to remain for the year. Books and stationery did not arrive because there was a printers' strike. The school office was in position just a fortnight before term started and Mr. Fletcher and his staff fought to get all clean and in place for the beginning of term. The author remembers similar chaos when the first extensions were built with no covered passage to the main school resulting in muddy, soaking feet traipsing through the school on wet days.

However, on September 12th 1956, the seven staff waited for the School to arrive. By 8.45 a.m. the two first forms and two second forms were 'dammed' behind the far cloakroom doors while the workmen retreated, hammering as they went pegs of wood into the metal frames to act as clothes pegs, since the proper hooks were lost somewhere on the way from Wolverhampton! The school was officially opened in 1957 and two years later came in a new influx of staff — of which the author was one — to cope with the senior work of the school. I think it is fair to say that this was a school where staff and girls worked as a team. The school was small enough for members of staff to know every girl and continuity reigned.

Many and varied were the activities with games, exhibitions, charity work and several clubs taking place in the lunch time. Plays were put on and here came the link with Price's with Sixth Form dances, joint plays and concerts. The school was to lose its sixth form and many of its staff to Price's when the latter became a Tertiary College. It is now Cams Hill School for boys and girls working to G.C.S.E.

FONTLEY SCHOOL - 1936

FONTLEY SCHOOL - 1938
Back row: includes Bloomfield, Wilks, Finland, Powell, Adams, Ford, Whitwick, Miller.
Middle row: includes Davidson, Ward, Menzies, Frost, Knight, Davidson, Turner.
Front row: Scrivens, Rance, Smith, Ward.

FONTLEY SCHOOL - 1954

CHURCH OF ENGLAND SCHOOL, GIRL'S CLASS - 1926

Back row: M. Garey, D. Alderslade, ?, A. Wheeler, V. Roffey, N. Newman, M. Kingswell, S. Candall, ?. 2nd row: D. Hutchings, D. Everett, M. Smith, E. Pumble, K. King, L. Clack, D. Bond, B. Wheeler, H. Evans, M. White, N. Gamblin. 3rd row: G. Clements, K. Wells, B. Tull, E. Coles, J. Cummings, E. Herridge, W. Carpenter, ?, J. Palmer, V. Duffett, P. Kinch, G. Etherington. Front row: K. Wise, M. Pearson, D. Weaver, ?, P. Wassell, N. Grant, D. Shutterling, B. Jacobs. Teacher, Miss Bundy, later married Mr. Smith, master at the Boys' School.

CHURCH OF ENGLAND SCHOOL, CLASS 1 - 1931

Back row: F. Lister, E. Rice, A. Tatford, S. Kenway, E. Miles, K. Bailey, J. Bright, ?, ?, D. Metcalfe. 2nd row: D. Webster, B. Hamel, L. Grafham, H. Cooper, J. Grigg, H. Hediker, Wassell, N. Bachelor, P. Lambeth, K. Champion. 3rd row: D. Fuller, K. Frost, J. Braschov, J. Stevens, S. Peckham, P. Middleton, P. Moor, K. Eggleton, B. Longford, B. Champion, E. Wheeler. 4th row: J. Legge, V. Herridge, J. Fuller, J. Light, J. Wheeler, G. Massey, H. Purver, P. Hopwood, K. Chance. Front row: H. Searle, B. Jarman, S. Rees, J. Bright, G. Rowe, F. Holbrook, G. Pierson.

FAREHAM CHURCH OF ENGLAND JUNIOR AND INFANTS' SCHOOL, CLASS 2 - 1933. Back row: Christopher Wright, Betty Moore, Joan Warner, Donald Wells, Betty Barker, Alec Gill. 2nd row: Barbara Watts, Roy Lacey, Rita Nutter, Morris Lemm, Iris Cottle, Madeline Thornton, Kathleen Wassell. 3rd row: Sidney Marsh, Beatrice Barnard, Walter Gee, Beatrice Batchelor, John Wrixon, Joyce Hayward. Seated in front: Marjorie Underwood, Mary Wassell.

CHURCH OF ENGLAND SCHOOL, CLASS IV - 1934

Back row: E. Barker, S. Rowe, J. Feast, H. Searle, M(?) Feast, F. Haslett, F. Brown, L. Jacobs. 2nd row: H. Buxey, J. Newland, E. Wheeler, L. Mitchell, E. Francis, F. Coker, J. Grigg, K. Chance (Teacher, Miss Cummins). 3rd row: F. Ridell, J. Legge, L. Mullins, Allen, K. Mulvaney, M. Feast, A. White, M. Fogarty, K. Bailey. 4th row: D. Davis, H. Everett, J. Light, J. Purver, V. Dicker, J. Figgins, D. Grigg, R. Turner. 5th row: J. Wright, A. Knight, R. Latty, D. Webster, R. Wassell, F. Holbrook, L. Laurence, L. King. Front row: V. Herridge, P. Birch, H. Moor, D. Curtis, M. Coles, B. Main, J. Vincent.

CHURCH OF ENGLAND SCHOOL, CLASS III - 1933

Back row: J. Legge, D. Metcalfe, E. Rice, M. Kinshott, J. Wright, E. Miles, H. Everett. 2nd row: K. Eggleton, J. Fuller, N. Bachelor, E. Barker, J. Swinburne, J. Braschov, F. Coker, K. Chance. 3rd row: Kenway, P. Hopgood, E. Wheeler, F. Holbrook, P. Lambeth, K. Bailey, J. Purver, F. Light, J. Hewlett. 4th row: A. Tatford, P. Moor, K. Champion, D. Fuller, B. Champion, J. Wheeler, J. Light, P. Middleton, J. Stevens. Front row: D. Webster, G. Rowe, H. Purver, V. Herridge, J. Grigg, G. Pierson, K. Frost, B. Jarman, A. Lamport.

WICKHAM ROAD SCHOOL JUNIORS - 1927
Those above include: V. Colwell, S. Bull, L. Collins, E. Pass, A. Ayling, C. Grant, W. Cox, D. Clark, N. Collins, D. Alderton, D. Mason.

WICKHAM ROAD JUNIOR SCHOOL - 1928
Those above include: E. Eames, H. Colebourne, A. Legg, E. Webber, D. Grafham, G. Hawkins, J. Smith, D. Alderton, W. Alderton, F. Hutchings, D. Clark, H. Spinks.

WICKHAM ROAD SCHOOL, 1934 – MISS JACKSON'S CLASS

Back row: D. Harbour, P. Meaton, ?, B. Bailey, P. Barton, M. Robinson, D. Walker, V. Eames. Middle row: B. Chamberlain, B. Colwell, K. McDonald, I. Adams, E. Colebourne, D. Harrison, A. Hedgecock, D. Adamson. Front row: P. Hoad, G. Phillips, H. Earwacker, P. Glover, F. Gnomes, P. Gamblin, H. Dawes, D. Broster.

WICKHAM ROAD JUNIOR SCHOOL – 1939

Back row: Richards, A. Elfeck, Mapson, J. Wylde, ?, L. Rowe, K. Verdison, P. Grace. 2nd row: Marnor, V. Painter, ?, G. Davison, ?, J. Cummings, Stannard, P. Holmes, ?. 3rd row: Golding, M. Hall, Bevis, R. Barlow, K. Clack, M. Winter, C. Clack, J. Wylde. Front row: Webb, J. Stapley, Alsford, B. Sergent, Adams.

WICKHAM ROAD JUNIOR SCHOOL, 1952 – H.M. Mr. Walker
Included above are: Susan Smith, Brian Hill, Christopher Hedges, Barry Sturmey, Catherine
Knight, Terry Keen, Christine Kirby, Barry Clark, Joan Swatton.

FAREHAM SECONDARY BOYS' SCHOOL, FORM IIIB.– 1949
Back row: H. Pink, Smith, C. Menzies, F. Watts. 2nd row: E. Walters, Read, D. Bulman,
J. Hand, ?, J. McKeown, M. Barnes. 3rd row: D. Cook, P. Gibbs, ?, M. Scruse, Ayling,
I. Osborne, R. Meredith. Front row: Mr. Smith (H.M.), Young, R. Elkins, B. Belcher,
C. Andrews, Paine, E. Wassell, Mr. Lanell.

106

HARRISON ROAD SENIOR GIRLS' SCHOOL, CLASS 1A – 1934
Teacher Miss Tribe.

FAREHAM SENIOR GIRLS' SCHOOL (Harrison Road), FORM 2A – Summer 1940
Back row: Trixie Damon. Brenda Rogers, Norah Langridge, Norah Randall, Doreen Harvey, Barbara Watts, Celia Haslam, Hazel Warnekey, Margaret Garrad, Molly Tainsh. 2nd row: Barbara Godfray, Ruby Harris, Evelyn Biggs, Rosemary Stead, Hazel Morris, Gwen Reed, Brenda Shawyer, Barbara Leonard, Sheila Tutt, Joan Stone, Sheila Knowles, Pauline Strawbridge. 3rd row: Audrey Sait, Betty Bradford, June Clark, Hilda Kercher, Pat Leal, Peggy Strugnell, Kathleen Wassell, Mary Wassell, Freda Daniels, Pauline Beer, Pamela Wright, Muriel Collins, Mollie Hutton. Front row: Betty Hopgood, Joyce Lee, Shirley Martin, Joyce Faithfull, Olive Russell, Mrs. Rothwell, Brenda West, Edna Phillips, Sylvia Brannan, Rona Coombes, Eileen Courtney, Joyce Hayward.

FONTLEY SCHOOL PLAY - 1944
Included in the above are: G. Stannard, G. Matthews, R. White, S. Phelps, E. Speed, R. Williams, M. Tune, C. Coombes, J. Harding, M. Rance, A. Jupe, L. Goodman.

FONTLEY SCHOOL PLAY - 1950s
(Note 'George Waters' string and paper carrier bag!)

War Time

A hotch-potch of personal memories. September 3rd 1939. So it was true. A brother in the Terriers had been called up on September 1st, and I sat on the arm of an armchair listening to the Prime Minister announcing that we were at war with Germany, an announcement closely followed by the sound of the air raid siren. Meanwhile, unknown to me, my future husband, as a boy telegraphist in HMS Belfast in the English Channel, received the message 'Commence hostilities with Germany'.

For the author, a teenager of eighteen and on the verge of University life, it seemed that nothing was ever going to be the same again and this indeed proved to be true. I had, with my contemporaries often discussed the possibilities of war, after all there had been the Spanish Civil War and the invasion of Abyssinia and it was obvious that things were happening in Germany. It was only too easy to realise that all our brothers would be involved. So we talked — how could women in Spain go about doing their shopping in the middle of a war — only to find out later that we would be doing the same and that life must go on, however scared we might be.

A race to put up blackout curtains and to criss-cross the windows with tape to check any possible blast. Sandbags and Anderson shelters or the space under the stairs to be strengthened. The weather was beautiful. Looking across the Creek to the 100-acre field of wheat waiting to be cut, it did not seem possible that there was a war on. Cinemas and theatres re-opened and we were in the middle of a so-called 'phoney war'.

Dunkirk. Dog fights overhead and a blessed Spitfire rolling back home the same way he had come to cheer us up. Night bombing, either fire watching or going to bed with one's head *under* the pillow! 'Don't tell me it's not a Jerry, I know that odd engine sound'.

Rationing, regular customers only, queues for unrationed goods or the unexpected luxury of an orange. I remember such a queue, at a fish shop on a sleety Good Friday. After three-quarters of an hour, the fish ran out and I returned home in tears. What *was* I going to make for a meal? No doubt the women behind me felt the same, but we coped.

The bombing of Portsmouth, dreadful nights. Not on duty so went to bed to be rudely awakened 'this is a dilly — you'll have to get up, put the kettle on for a cup of tea'. England's salvation indeed! Incendiaries all over the place, many kicked into the Creek to save time and the Sailing Club launch did not float on the rising tide, a casualty of war.

Up to Cambridge the next day, a struggle through Gosport to the ferry, no Harbour Station! A group of us followed our noses to try to find the Town Station. No use asking and no familiar buildings to guide us, just rubble, ruins and the beginnings of the smell of a bombed town. Don't dare ask the name of the railway station — make sure you count the stops. Blackout, of course, meant two or was it three — pieces of tissue paper inside one's bike lamp. Firewatching, lectures, a realisation that several of the men undergraduates were no longer there, the peace of the countryside in the early evening and the bombers taking off. We counted them out and, lying in bed, counted them back.

Fruit picking in the summer vacations — double summer time, so being out in the strawberry fields at 5 a.m. really meant 3 a.m. Two hours later, the sun rose . . . ! We paid our own fares, did an eight-hour day, were paid 38 shillings a week and had to give back 20 shillings for our keep. Deep in the countryside meant no hot water and earth closets! It was compulsory. Telegram home — 'I need a bath!' Bliss, even if we were allowed only five inches of water in the bath. Long arguments — five inches when you were in the bath or five inches when you were out of the bath?

The 'Hood' sunk and the news travelled like wildfire. Anxious women came out to their back gates. Too many sailors from the local area this time. The 'Graf Spee' being chased, the chase followed by everyone, then the 'Altmark' and 'the Navy's here!' Memories do not have a chronological order, one leads to another.

Struggling to do local history for a thesis, when all the old maps were in the filthy cellars (dungeons?) at the Castle, Winchester and cycling home covered in this filth. Three signatures needed if you wanted those precious six-inch maps. They all had the forts carefully blotted out — so carefully that there was a white space of exactly the right size and shape where the missing fort should have been! Identity Card to be carried at all times, never once did I have to show it, I must have looked too English!

Army Smoke Makers (nicknamed 'soup kitchens') would line up along the Gosport Road. The idea was to blot out the harbour but somehow the wind always changed direction and the houses got the lot. Trying to get round clothes rationing, we bought up thick darning wool to knit until some wretched department caught on and the wool was cut into short lengths!

Dieppe, Canadians everywhere, waiting for embarkation. Little did the author know that a childhood friend was among them. The air raid siren sounded early, all remained quiet and we went to the pictures just as a Heinkel strafed West Street and we dived for shop doorways — but we still went to the pictures at the Savoy. But we came out to find that all had gone hideously wrong and the ambulances were rushing down the Gosport Road. Reality again forced itself upon us.

The arrival of a precious food parcel from America. A tin of pineapple chunks! Surely my young nephew would not like pineapple, never having tasted it!

We watched greedily and hopefully — but he did! But his grandmother's description of a banana and how you peeled it was met with hysterical disbelief. A small turkey for Christmas (grey market!). The remains on Boxing Day carefully rationed and put on plates in the dining room. Enter the family; no turkey. A true case of 'your dinner is in the dog!'

D. Day. The skies full of planes, the 'alert' on but no German planes. The roads full of troops and vehicles the like of which one had never seen before, moving down Portland Street and Quay Street nose to tail. The noise as one pressed oneself close to the buildings, was deafening and the houses shook. The troops moved to the embarkation points, obviously for a practice run, then came back and quite suddenly were gone again, to be replaced by a further group as the invasion continued.

There were other things to contend with. There were now V1s or 'doodle bugs' and Fareham had its share. The author was now teaching in the East End of London where V1s were common. Then came the V2s, shattering to the nerves when one had felt sure that one was through the war safely. There was nothing you could do about them. If you didn't hear one, you were dead. Yet they had their amusing moments as when two of us and the dog dived under the small kitchen table and the dog got there first. But finally one fell by the school, fortunately ten minutes before the children arrived for the blast blew glass into all the classrooms. It did indeed seem a miracle.

VE Day, no blackouts, lights streaming out and rejoicing and street parties everywhere. Yet even after fifty years, there are too many memories almost too hard to bear and there was still VJ Day to wait for. Rationing got worse, not better, austerity was the order of the day and this went on for several years. Life truly was never the same again. Personal recollections, anyone of my age has similar ones. Older people probably had even more to bear. Some memories will be happpier and some infinitely more tragic. It was World War II.

It was obvious to most people well before 1939 that war was inevitable. Certainly in 1937, it was 'action stations' as far as the Fareham Fire Brigade was concerned. Arthur Sutton, the Chief Fire Officer went on record to say that they needed to recruit 54 Auxiliary Firemen over the age of forty and twenty fire wardens to man specific posts across the area in order to assist householders. In the event of telephone communications breaking down, he said 'Boy Scouts and members of the Boys' Brigade should be enrolled as messenger cyclists.' He would also need 'another ladder, cost £19 10s.' The demand quickly grew and the Air Raid Precautions Committee (A.R.P.) under Captain Manley Power asked for 520 men and 200 women volunteers.

In the middle of all these preparations, Mr. A. A. Reader, the Second Officer died suddenly. This was a sad loss to the Fire Brigade as well as to Fareham. He was the son of Mr. C. Reader, the 'father' of the Fire Brigade. In 1938,

Leading Fireman Freeman with Firewomen (left to right) Enid Fryer, Vi Diaper, Sylvia Munday, Beryl Lawrence and Jonhy Jonstone – 1943.

Mr. A. Sutton retired after fifty years service, but he continued to take a great interest in 'his' Fire Brigade.

Munich in 1938 gave a breathing space, but preparations went ahead. Sandbags, Anderson air raid shelters and blackout materials made their appearance. War came and with it Identity Cards, Ration Books and later Clothing Coupons. The Local Defence Volunteers (L.D.V.) came into being with small groups drilling using any 'weapons' that might be to hand. They were to become the Home Guard (frequently known these days as Dad's Army). Nor were the exploits of Dad's Army on television particularly exaggerated. Fareham and its surroundings had several companies which met regularly and had joint exercises. Such was the case when Knowle Hospital Staff took on Fontley. Fontley Base H.Q. just happened to be the 'Miners Arms' and it was not long before the message was signalled to their Home Guard 'take no more prisoners'. The enemy were drinking the 'Miners Arms' dry! Mr. F. Cook tells a true story of a pilot parachuting down into Fontley. Men rushed to the scene doubtless with any farming implement available. The pilot was captured — but what were they to do with him? So he was placed in the telephone kiosk and the *kiosk* was roped up! So how was it going to be possible to inform anyone officially by telephone? Fortunately he turned out to be a 'friend' even though a foreigner. Was he one of our Polish allies?

Fareham Pre-War Volunteer Fire Service at their headquarters (Mayling House, Highlands Road). Front right is B. Phelps.

Auxiliary Fire Service at Mayling House, 1943.

113

KNOWLE HOME GUARD (All were members of Knowle Hospital Staff)
Back row: E. Randle, A. Ford, Naylor, W. Berry, J. Burr. 2nd row: G. Freeman, Foster,
Thorp, C. Towler, M. Rochford, Woods, Collins. 3rd row: A. Watts, Marshall, Moss,
Thomas, Hocking, Bowers, Green. Front row: W. Ware, W. Pope, L. Cunliff.

The large houses were taken over, usually by the forces. The Royal Navy took over the 'Old Manor House' in Wickham Road for the WRNS. Fort Wallington became a naval and WRNS quarters. Roche Court and Kneller Court were occupied by the Services, Blackbrook Farm became a store and repair depot. Cams Halls was also commandeered by the Admiralty in 1941 to house the Manager Engineering Department Drawing Office after the original office was blitzed in 1941. They were to keep control until 1949.

Like other towns, Fareham put its back into the war effort. Buying a fighter plane at the cost of £5,000 became its objective in 1940 and by November they had raised £2,000, the amount being announced at the end of a special football match against Portsmouth.

HMS Collingwood came into being in 1939. Built originally as a 'New Entry Training Establishment for Special Reserve Ratings' it was built on a marshy, waterlogged site once described as 'the best snipe marsh in the country'. It started as a collection of huts and it was to expand rapidly, finally taking in 10,000 men. The WRNS joined from the start. The establishment was to 'er from enemy raids. An alert in July, 1940, occurred when King George VI was on a visit although there was no attack. But a few months later a stick of bombs straddled the road, one damaging the theatre, the other two

Even in war-time events such as the Wallington Carnival went on.

Below: A.R.P. practice in Fareham's High Street.

failing to explode. In early 1941, the camp was attacked during 'Divisions'. Worst of all was the bomb in 1943 resulting in the death of thirty ratings.

'Collingwood' was always a morale booster with its Saturday march through the town. It also had its domestic side in its vegetable gardens and its piggeries. (Rumour has it, that at one Wardroom Mess Dinner, the hall doors were opened and several very young piglets were let loose among the diners, squealing as they went. The WRNS waitresses fled in terror as several unsuccessful attempts were made to corner the piglets.)

Sticks of bombs were to straddle Fareham and cause loss of life and one waited nightly for the sirens, the guns and the bombers. Was it going to be Portsmouth or Southampton? If the latter, one was sufficiently hardened to go to bed, feeling that at least one might as well die in comfort. All old Farehamites will have these and other memories. A relation of Mr. A. Sutton, meticulously recorded every alert and raid for 1940 until he was killed with his family on November 6th.

To return to Cams Hall. Mrs. Bell remembers the striking features of the Hall at that time, features which were never to return. The famous fireplaces were covered in for protection. The Department became self sufficient with a generator room and its own telephone switchboard room and its administrative and clerical staff, most of whom came in from Portsmouth. There was a barrage balloon site and eventually Marine Commandos encamped there before D Day. Design work for the conversion of major liners into depot repair ships was carried out here. Later, the conversion plans for the post-war cruise of King George VI in HMS Vanguard were done at the same office. Austerity prevailed — drawing paper was used on both sides!

Miss Aisher's base was the Telephone Room where she took turns on the switchboard. She was responsible for distributing Dockyard papers twice daily to all the offices and also took the post to Fareham (often changing the bosses' library books at Boots library). She remembers the Marines at bayonet practice and the beauty of the now derelict house. There were four in the phone room; one girl, half French, had lost touch with her relations but there was to be a happy ending as some of the Marines successfully traced her family. There were quiet Sunday duties, cups of tea, fortune telling from the tea leaves and forbidden games of cards! The discarded drawings on linen also came in handy because after a thorough wash they emerged pure white and were used for embroidered tray cloths.

Many families gave hospitality to Servicemen in the district as, of course, did regular organisations. Mrs. Slater, daughter of Sidney Smith the photographer, remembers the war years at 88 West Street. 'An horrific time, but also happy as the front door was always open to all Service men and men, usually from Collingwood. The big room over the shop was used for dancing, parties and games.' There were social evenings at the 'Red Lion' and the 'Cedar Cafe'.

The wonderful excitement of the end of the war – with a fabulous street party in Paxton Road.

So came VE Day, no blackouts and street parties organised with special streets closed to traffic. The European war was over. The waiting for VJ Day seemed endless for many families. Life, however, in spite of austerity settled down to some semblance of normality.

Changes were now happening in Fareham, the market town was expanding, estates were growing and the port was dying. Fareham also was never, for good or ill going to be the same again.

Below: Another V.E. party with the happy families·of Trinity Street celebrating behind the Church Hall.

The Bedenham explosion.

We cannot close this book without mentioning that peace and tranquillity were rudely shaken on July 14th 1950, when the Bedenham explosion occurred. There had been recurring sounds of exploding ammunition and police came ...d warning people to open doors and windows. Then came the big explosion ... a cloud rising to about 4,000 feet. People were blown off their bicycles, ...ts, ceilings and windows were shattered and as the blast funnelled up the ...d up Hartlands Road, Quay Street and Portland Street, the glass was ...ut of every window in West Street. It might be said to have been a ...script to wartime.

June, 1953 – the children of Fontley (and their parents) are faced with the 'serious' business of celebrating the Coronation of Queen Elizabeth II. They had a wonderful Coronation Carnival.

Conclusion

Reaching the end of this book I can only say that once again I have been overwhelmed by the amount of material that has had to be left out. There are topics begging for inclusion which have not even been touched upon — the Turnpikes, the Churches, and the modern schools, the farms around the area and the ironworks of Henry Cort. Then there are the big houses and their families, the Parkers at Blackbrook, Jellicoe and Beardmore at 'Uplands and the Delmes at Cams, to name but a few. There is much to be said about the Fire Brigade, the numerous local societies like the Brotherhood, the Oddfellows and the Foresters. There are also the Music, Dramatic, Sailing and Athletic societies.

Above all, there are the many memories from the modern, reaching through grandparents to the late 1800s. All these go to weave the tapestry which is Fareham and no-one is more conscious than the author that the threads have only just been set up upon the loom. This, after more than thirty of serious research!.

Acknowledgements

It is impossible to name everyone with whom I have chatted about Fareham or who has let slip some vital information without realising it. Most of the postcards and photographs are from my own collection. Some Farehamites are mentioned in the text but here are the names of others to whom I am indebted:-

Mr. Akers
The Rev. W. Alder
Mrs. Baxandall
Mrs. Bell
Mrs. Billett
Mrs. Bowers
Mrs. Budd
Mr. Bulman
Mrs. Cantle
Mrs. Clapperton
Mr. and Mrs. Clark
Mr. Cook
Mrs. Clifton
Miss Crawshaw
Mr. Etherington
Mr. Ford
Mr. Gamblin
Mr. Grant
Mr. D. Hayward
Mr. K. Hayward
Mrs. Harper
Mrs. Hartley
Mr. Hoare
Miss Jelley
Mrs. .....ery
Mrs. Jones

Lawrence & Sons
Mrs. Lawrence
Mr. Lees
Mrs. Leppard
Mr. Mott
Mrs. Mouland
Mrs. Newton
Mr. Privett
Mrs. Race
Mr. J. Race
Mr. Sanders
Mrs. Shawyer
Mr. K. Shawyer
Mrs. Shepherd
Mrs. Smith (Fontley)
Mrs. (Phelps) Smith
Mr. Stock
Mr. A. Sturgess
Mr. H. Sturgess
Mr. Swatton
Mr. Swinburne
Mr. Tyrell
Mr. Worlock
Mrs. Worsfield
Mrs. Yoxall

Special thanks to Mr. Alastair Penfold (Curator, Westbury Manor Museum).

Last but not least, my husband for his typing and genius for 'getting things in order'.

A.J.